California
Bar
Examination

Performance Tests
and
Selected Answers

February 2012

PERFORMANCE TESTS AND SELECTED ANSWERS
FEBRUARY 2012
CALIFORNIA BAR EXAMINATION

This publication contains two performance tests from the February 2012 California Bar Examination and two selected answers to each test.

The answers received good grades and were written by applicants who passed the examination. The answers were produced as submitted, except that minor corrections in spelling and punctuation were made for ease in reading. The answers are reproduced here with the consent of their authors.

Contents

Performance Test A
INSTRUCTIONS AND FILE

IN RE SWAYNE

IN RE SWAYNE

INSTRUCTIONS

1. This performance test is designed to evaluate your ability to handle a select number of legal authorities in the context of a factual problem involving a client.

2. The problem is set in the fictional State of Columbia, one of the United States.

3. You will have two sets of materials with which to work: a File and a Library.

4. The File contains factual materials about your case. The first document is a memorandum containing the instructions for the tasks you are to complete.

5. The Library contains the legal authorities needed to complete the tasks. The case reports may be real, modified, or written solely for the purpose of this performance test. If the cases appear familiar to you, do not assume that they are precisely the same as you have read before. Read each thoroughly, as if it were new to you. You should assume that cases were decided in the jurisdictions and on the dates shown. In citing cases from the Library, you may use abbreviations and omit page citations.

6. You should concentrate on the materials provided, but you should also bring to bear on the problem your general knowledge of the law. What you have learned in law school and elsewhere provides the general background for analyzing the problem; the File and Library provide the specific materials with which you must work.

7. Although there are no restrictions on how you apportion your time, you should probably allocate at least 90 minutes to reading and organizing before you begin preparing your response.

8. Your response will be graded on its compliance with instructions and on its content, thoroughness, and organization.

Arbuckle Baines, LLP
Attorneys at Law
Walkerville, Columbia

INTEROFFICE MEMORANDUM

TO: Applicant

FROM: Roger Arbuckle

DATE: February 28, 2012
SUBJECT: Law Offices of Richard Swayne – Business Plan

Our client, Richard Swayne, is a lawyer who practices law here in Walkerville as a solo practitioner. A college classmate of his, Ann Moulton, has proposed that she and Mr. Swayne enter into a business arrangement, which would be to publish and market a series of legal forms for use by individuals and small business entities wishing to represent themselves rather than retain counsel.

Ms. Moulton has presented Mr. Swayne with a business plan that spells out the scope and contours of the proposed business arrangement. He has some concerns about the legal ethics of entering into such an arrangement and has asked us to advise him on that aspect of the venture.

Please draft a two-part memorandum to prepare me for my upcoming meeting with Mr. Swayne.

In Part 1, explain what specific ethical problems the following parts of the Business Plan present under the Columbia Rules of Professional Conduct and the Professions Code:

1. Each of the duties of the "receptionist" listed in the "helpline" service section of the plan.

2. The revenue sharing arrangements described in the plan.

3. The partnership nature of the venture.

In Part 2, explain the following:

4. Whether Swayne's drafting the forms and instructions constitute "law-related services" and, if so, what Swayne's ethical obligations are to the users of the forms.

5. What obligation, if any, Swayne might have to supervise the "receptionist."

There are several other ethical issues that I have assigned to another associate to explore. You should focus only on the ones I've listed above.

1 **Transcript of Interview with Richard ("Dick") Swayne**

2 **February 27, 2012**

3   * * *

4 **Roger Arbuckle:** Hi, Dick. I'm glad you could come in to talk about that business plan

5 you told me about over the phone yesterday. Did you bring it with you?

6 **Richard Swayne:** Yeah, I did. Here it is.

7 **Arbuckle:** Great. I'll take a close look at it later, but let's talk so you can at least give

8 me the highlights.

9 **Swayne:** OK. It's a business venture I'd really like to do, but I want to be sure I don't

10 run into any ethical problems. Basically, Ann Moulton – she's a college acquaintance of

11 mine – did some market research and found that there are lots of individuals and small

12 business owners who don't want to spend the money on an attorney to handle relatively

13 minor legal problems. She came up with the idea of putting together sets of legal forms

14 that litigants can buy and use to do the work themselves. I'd draft the forms and the

15 instructions. Ann would handle the marketing and sales, mainly over the Internet.

16 **Arbuckle:** Describe your existing practice for me.

17 **Swayne:** It's a small but busy practice, mostly plaintiff's personal injury cases – car

18 accidents, product liability, slip-and-falls – that sort of thing. I also represent debtors

19 against creditors' claims and small business owners in commercial disputes. Probably

20 about one-fifth of my work involves estate matters – wills, probate, uncomplicated estate

21 planning. I'm a solo practitioner, so on larger, complicated matters, I usually associate

22 co-counsel with special expertise.

23 **Arbuckle:** What sort of business association would you operate this new venture

24 under?

25 **Swayne:** We'd form a limited liability partnership. Ann would be the general partner

26 responsible for running the day-to-day operations, and I'd be the limited partner. We'd

27 share the profits and losses 50-50.

28 **Arbuckle:** I see. Well, do you think there's enough money in such a venture to make it

29 worth your while?

30 **Swayne:** I *think* so. We're estimating that it will begin generating profits in the fourth or

31 fifth year, but there are some immediate side advantages to me.

32 **Arbuckle:** Like what?

1   **Swayne:** Well, first of all, I own the building on Center Street, and my law offices now

2   occupy only half of it. The new LLP would lease the other half from me. Second, aside

3   from my share from the sales of the forms, I'd get a lot of referrals and client leads that I

4   could follow up on and use to develop my law business. Of course, as you can see in

5   the plan, I'd have to share with the LLP some of the referral fees. But, all told, it would

6   represent a nice piece of change.

7   **Arbuckle:** I'd want to take a very close look at those aspects of the deal before you

8   agree to any of that.

9   **Swayne:** Why? Those are the parts of the deal that make it worthwhile to me.

10   **Arbuckle:** Because I think some of that comes pretty close to crossing the ethical line.

11   Would any of your office staff be involved in running the LLP?

12   **Swayne:** No, not really. The LLP would hire its own staff, including the receptionist,

13   who would be the main contact point for those who email or call in by phone. Although I

14   guess I'd be available to answer any questions if a user of the forms wanted to contact

15   me.

16   **Arbuckle:** Give me an example of what kinds of questions you're talking about.

17   **Swayne:** Well, I mean things that don't involve my professional judgment, like where to

18   file, how many copies, what are the filing fees, and so forth.

19   **Arbuckle:** What exactly would be the receptionist's duties?

20   **Swayne:** That person's duties are pretty well spelled out in the business plan, at least

21   insofar as they relate to the LLP. But that person would also direct clients of mine who

22   come in for appointments or consultations to me. And, I guess, if a user of the forms

23   called in or walked in and had a question for me, the receptionist would direct that

24   person to me as well. The business plan has a provision that would allow the users of

25   the forms to refer questions to me and to contact me for limited free consultations.

26   **Arbuckle:** What do you mean "limited?"

27   **Swayne:** I'm not quite sure. I'd answer simple questions for free, but if it got beyond

28   simple information, for example into issues of liability or strategy that require my

29   professional judgment, I'd handle the person as a regular client of my firm and bill him

30   or her as usual for my services.

31   **Arbuckle:** Is there going to be just a single phone number so that all calls for both you

32   and the LLP will be routed through the receptionist?

1 **Swayne:** No. I'll have my own phone number for my law office, and calls related to my

2 law practice will be routed directly to me.

3 **Arbuckle:** I'd want to take a close look at those things too. Would you have any

4 supervisory role or authority over the receptionist?

5 **Swayne:** Not if I could help it. I just don't want to divert my energies to running the LLP

6 and being held to the duties of a general partner. As far as I'm concerned, Ann alone

7 will be supervising the receptionist. As you know, under the LLP laws, the general

8 partner is completely responsible and liable, unless a limited partner gets involved in

9 managing the day-to-day affairs.

10 **Arbuckle:** That's right, but, as *you* know, that doesn't preclude the application of the

11 Rules of Professional Conduct to you. But tell me a little bit about what your role would

12 be in creating the forms and instructions for their use.

13 **Swayne:** Well, it would be the usual range of forms used in commencing litigation and

14 responding to litigation already commenced – summons, complaints, answers,

15 discovery documents, motions, and the like. Then, I'd draft the instructions on what

16 forms to use for specific purposes.

17 **Arbuckle:** Would these instructions contain any directions or suggestions about what

18 language the user should employ to fill in spaces on the forms where narrative

19 statements are required?

20 **Swayne:** No. The instructions would simply tell them what boxes to check and spaces

21 to fill out, without telling them what language to use. They would also explain the filing

22 requirements. I wouldn't want it to appear that I am giving legal advice to the users of

23 the forms by telling them what language to use. I'd leave that part of it up to the

24 receptionist when users contact him or her for assistance.

25 **Arbuckle:** Anything else that I should be aware of?

26 **Swayne:** No. Ann and I have discussed the various ways we can structure this. For

27 example, in the original draft of the business plan, in my capacity as a lawyer – not as a

28 member of the LLP – I would have been retained as the lawyer for the LLP to handle

29 any legal matters and claims against the partnership, and I'd charge the LLP my usual

30 rates. I rejected that idea. I want a cleaner relationship and one with greater financial

31 potential. I want to be a partner of an LLP, not an employee, consultant, independent

32 contractor, or anything else.

1   **Arbuckle:** OK. I hope that can be accomplished under the rules, but maybe not. By

2   the way, do you want advice or help from me on the technicalities of formation of the

3   LLP?

4   **Swayne:** No. I can take care of that myself.

5   **Arbuckle:** All right, then. Give me a few days to do the research, and I'll get back to

6   you.

7   **Swayne:** Thanks, Roger. I'll be anxious to hear from you.

Business Plan

Self-Help Legal Enterprise Project, LLP

OVERVIEW: Research shows that there are many small business entities and individuals in the State of Columbia and elsewhere who choose to represent themselves in litigation and related legal matters rather than retain counsel. There is a need for legal forms that conform to the rules of the courts of the State of Columbia, such as will enable such persons to comply with filing and pleading requirements. The undertaking proposed in this Plan will fill that need and, at the same time, serve as a business development vehicle for both the sale of such forms and the law practice of participating lawyers.

Form of the undertaking: This Plan contemplates the creation of a limited liability partnership named Self-Help Legal Enterprise Project, LLP (SHLEP).

<u>General Partner</u>: Ann Moulton, BS, MBA, University of Columbia, will be the managing partner and will manage the day-to-day operations of the partnership. Ms. Moulton was formerly employed as Regional Vice President and Sales Manager of Manifold Business Forms, Inc., a nationwide producer and supplier of business forms. As such, Ms. Moulton has an existing business network that will facilitate production and marketing of SHLEP's legal forms.

<u>Limited Partner</u>: Richard Swayne, BA, JD, University of Columbia, will be the sole limited partner. Mr. Swayne has been a practicing lawyer in the City of Walkerville, Columbia for 15 years. He is a solo practitioner. He has familiarity with the court system and the requisites necessary to ensure that the forms will comply with court rules.

<u>Office Facilities</u>: The current law offices of Richard Swayne are located in a building at 42 Center Street owned by Mr. Swayne. Swayne and his staff are currently the sole occupants of the building. This Plan contemplates that the west wing of the building, which is currently vacant, would be leased from Swayne and occupied by SHLEP and its staff at a rental amount to be determined and paid to Swayne. The east wing would continue to be occupied by The Law Offices of Richard Swayne.

Contribution of Capital and Division of Profits and Losses: Ann Moulton and Richard Swayne shall each contribute $100,000 in cash at the inception of SHLEP and, thereafter, their skill and labor and such other amounts of capital as shall be necessary. Ms. Moulton and Mr. Swayne shall share profits and losses equally.

Method of Operation: To the extent permitted by law, SHLEP and The Law Offices of Richard Swayne shall work cooperatively to maximize the sale and use of the legal forms produced and marketed by SHLEP. There shall be the following division of labor between the two entities.

Production of Legal Forms: Mr. Swayne shall be primarily responsible for determining the types of forms that are necessary and the design thereof to ensure compliance with the rules of the courts of the State of Columbia. He shall also be responsible for drafting instructions for the use and purposes of the forms in any advertising and marketing media utilized by SHLEP.

Ms. Moulton shall be primarily responsible for contracting with printers for printing, packaging, and purchasing paper forms, taking orders for, and shipping forms to purchasers who wish to use hard copy rather than online features, and for designing and implementing website access for online completion of the forms and court filing.

Marketing and Sales: The principal means of marketing and utilizing the forms will be via a SHLEP website on the Internet and advertising in legal publications. Ms. Moulton, as general partner of SHLEP, shall be responsible for such advertising and the creation and maintenance of a SHLEP website. All costs of advertising, marketing, and sales shall be borne by SHLEP. The advertising and website shall promote use of the forms and shall contain the following features:

- Descriptions of the various forms and their uses, emphasizing that they are accompanied by a complete set of written instructions for completion and filing of the forms.
- Representations that the forms and instructions were created by Richard Swayne, an experienced attorney licensed in the State of Columbia, including assurances that the forms, if properly filled out and filed, will comply with court rules.
- A schedule showing the cost of the forms and quantity discounts.
- A mechanism for online ordering and paying for the forms, requiring the potential purchaser to provide name, address, and telephone number and offering the option of paying by credit card.

- Emphasis on the security and confidentiality of the website and "online" capabilities for completion and filing of the forms with the courts.

- A "helpline" telephone number that purchasers of the forms can call for free-of-charge assistance in completing the forms and directions for filing them.

- Email capability for users to attach completed forms to be checked by the receptionist for completeness and to ask and get responses to questions.

- A link to the court system for online, electronic filing and service of the forms with the courts.

- A representation that Mr. Swayne is available for free limited consultation to any user of SHLEP's forms.

- An email link, which the caller can click and use to send a question or other inquiry to SHLEP and/or Mr. Swayne.

Free "Helpline" Service: SHLEP shall hire a receptionist. The duties of the receptionist shall include the following:

- The receptionist will answer telephones and greet customers of SHLEP.

- The receptionist will take all "helpline" calls and assist the callers in filling out the forms by answering their questions, telling them which boxes to check, and helping to formulate language to be inserted in various parts of the forms.

- The receptionist will respond to all email inquiries received from users of the forms.

- The receptionist shall also screen all callers and make an initial determination whether the caller needs legal assistance beyond mere help in filling out the forms.   If so, the receptionist shall so inform the caller and tell the caller that Mr. Swayne is available for immediate consultation for $250. If the caller agrees to pay for a consultation, the receptionist shall transfer the call to Mr. Swayne.

- The receptionist shall maintain records of the names, addresses, and telephone numbers of all "helpline" callers and, monthly, shall furnish said records to The Law Offices of Richard Swayne as "leads" Mr. Swayne may wish to pursue for client development purposes.

<u>Books of Account and Sharing of Revenues</u>: SHLEP and The Law Offices of Richard Swayne shall in all respects maintain separate financial records, books of account, payroll, accounts receivable and payable, and bank accounts and, with the following exceptions, shall each bear its own expenses and costs of operation.

- SHLEP and The Law Offices of Richard Swayne shall pay equally all costs of utilities, telephone and high-speed Internet services.

- SHLEP shall pay Richard Swayne from the revenues of SHLEP the agreed-upon lease rental for the office facilities on Center Street.

- Mr. Swayne shall remit to SHLEP 50% of all consultation fees he receives from callers referred to him by the receptionist.

- The Law Offices of Richard Swayne shall remit to SHLEP 10% of all fees earned from "leads" obtained from the receptionist.

- Mr. Swayne shall reimburse one-half of the cost of health insurance and other fringe benefits provided to the receptionist.

[Financial Projections Omitted]

Performance Test A
LIBRARY

IN RE SWAYNE

LIBRARY

Selected Provisions of Columbia Rules of Professional Conduct

Rule 1-100. Rules of Professional Conduct, in General: The Columbia Rules, together with any standards adopted by the Board of Governors pursuant to these rules, shall be binding upon all lawyers admitted to practice by the State Bar of Columbia.

Lawyers are also bound by the applicable case law and the provisions of the Columbia Professions Code. Although not binding, opinions of ethics committees in Columbia and other jurisdictions and bar associations should be consulted by lawyers for guidance on proper professional conduct.

*　　*　　*

Rule 1-120. Assisting, Soliciting, or Inducing Violations: A lawyer shall not knowingly assist in, solicit, or induce any violation of these rules or the Columbia Professions Code.

*　　*　　*

Rule 1-300. Unauthorized Practice of Law: A lawyer shall not aid any person or entity in the unauthorized practice of law.

*　　*　　*

Rule 1-310. Forming a Partnership with a Non-Lawyer: A lawyer shall not form a partnership with a person who is not a lawyer if any of the activities of that partnership consist of the practice of law.

Discussion: Rule 1-310 is not intended to govern lawyers' activities that cannot be considered to constitute the practice of law. It is intended solely to preclude a lawyer from being involved in the practice of law with a person who is not a lawyer.

*　　*　　*

13

Rule 1-320. Financial Arrangements with Non-Lawyers: (A) Neither a lawyer nor a law firm shall directly or indirectly share legal fees with a person who is not a lawyer.

(B) A lawyer shall not compensate, give, or promise anything of value to any person or entity for the purpose of recommending or securing employment of the lawyer or the lawyer's law firm by a client, or as a reward for having made a recommendation resulting in employment of the lawyer or the lawyer's law firm by a client.

* * *

Rule 1-400. Solicitation: For purposes of this rule, a "solicitation" means any communication concerning the availability for professional employment of a lawyer or a law firm in which a significant motive is pecuniary gain and that is delivered in person or by telephone. A solicitation shall not be made by or on behalf of a lawyer or law firm to a prospective client with whom the lawyer or law firm has no family or prior professional relationship, unless the solicitation is protected from abridgment by the Constitution of the United States or by the Constitution of the State of Columbia.

* * *

Rule 1-500. Responsibilities Regarding Non-Lawyer Assistants: With respect to a non-lawyer employed or retained by or associated with a lawyer:

(A) A lawyer who possesses managerial authority in a law firm shall make reasonable efforts to ensure that the firm has in effect measures giving reasonable assurance that the person's conduct is compatible with the professional obligations of the lawyer;

(B) A lawyer having direct supervisory authority over the non-lawyer shall make reasonable efforts to ensure that the person's conduct is compatible with the professional obligations of the lawyer.

* * *

Discussion: Lawyers generally employ assistants in their practice, including secretaries, investigators, law student interns, and paraprofessionals. Such assistants, whether

14

employees or independent contractors, act for the lawyer in rendition of the lawyer's professional services. A lawyer must give such assistants appropriate instruction and supervision concerning the ethical aspects of their employment, particularly regarding the obligation not to disclose information relating to representation of the client, and should be responsible for their work product. The measures employed in supervising non-lawyers should take account of the fact that they do not have legal training and are not subject to professional discipline.

*　　*　　*

Rule 1-600. Responsibilities Regarding Law-Related Services: (A) The term "law-related services" denotes services that might reasonably be performed in conjunction with and in substance are related to the provision of legal services, and that are not prohibited as unauthorized practice of law when provided by a non-lawyer.

(B) A lawyer shall be subject to the Rules of Professional Conduct with respect to the provision of law-related services, as defined in paragraph (A), if the law-related services are provided:

> (1) by the lawyer in circumstances that are not distinct from the lawyer's provision of legal services to clients; or

> (2) in other circumstances by an entity controlled by the lawyer individually or with others if the lawyer fails to take reasonable measures to assure that a person obtaining the law-related services knows that the services are not legal services and that the protections of the client-lawyer relationship do not exist.

Discussion: "Law–related services" and "legal services" are two distinct things. Rule 1-600 applies to the provision of law-related services by a lawyer even when the lawyer does not provide any legal services to the person for whom the law-related services are performed and regardless of whether the law-related services are performed through a law firm or a separate entity. The conduct of a lawyer involved in the provision of law-related services is subject to those Rules that apply generally to lawyer conduct, regardless of whether the conduct involves the provision of legal services.

If the lawyer individually or with others has control of such an entity's operations, the Rule requires the lawyer to take reasonable measures to assure that each person using the services of the entity knows that the services provided by the entity are not legal services and that the Rules of Professional Conduct that relate to the client-lawyer relationship do not apply. A lawyer's control of an entity extends to the ability to direct its operation. Whether a lawyer has such control will depend upon the circumstances of the particular case.

Regardless of the sophistication of potential recipients of law-related services, a lawyer should take special care to keep separate the provision of law-related and legal services in order to minimize the risk that the recipient will assume that the law-related services are legal services. The lawyer must take reasonable measures to communicate a clear, understandable disclaimer to assure that the recipient of the law-related services knows that the services are not legal services and the protections of the client-lawyer relationship do not apply.

Selected Provisions of Columbia Professions Code

Section 25. Practice of Law: The practice of law is the provision of legal services. It includes, but is not limited to, giving any kind of advice, explanation, opinion, or recommendation to a consumer about possible legal rights, remedies, defenses, options, selection of forms, or strategies. No person shall practice law in Columbia unless the person is an active lawyer of the State Bar.

* * *

Section 51. Runner or Capper: As used in this article:

A runner or capper is any person, firm, association or corporation acting for consideration in any manner or in any capacity as an agent for an attorney-at-law or law firm, whether the attorney or any lawyer of the law firm is admitted in Columbia or any other jurisdiction, in the solicitation or procurement of business for the attorney-at-law or law firm as provided in this article. An agent is one who represents another in dealings with one or more third persons.

Section 52. Prohibited Solicitations by Runner or Capper: (a) It is unlawful for:
Any person, in an individual capacity or in a capacity as a public or private employee, or for any firm, corporation, partnership or association to act as a runner or capper for any attorneys or to solicit any business for any attorneys in and about the state prisons, county jails, city jails, city prisons, or other places of detention of persons, city receiving hospitals, city and county receiving hospitals, county hospitals, superior courts, or in any public institution or in any public place or upon any public street or highway.

* * *

Section 64. Self-Help Services Provided by Legal Document Assistants:
(a) **" Legal document assistant"** means any person, corporation, partnership, association, or other entity that provides, or assists in providing, or offers to provide, or offers to assist in providing, for compensation, any self-help service to a member of the public who is representing himself or herself in a legal matter, or who holds himself or

17

herself out as someone who offers that service or has that authority. This paragraph does not apply to any individual whose assistance consists merely of secretarial or receptionist services.

(b) **"Self-help service"** means all of the following:

(1) Completing legal documents in a ministerial manner, selected by a person who is representing himself or herself in a legal matter, by typing or otherwise completing the documents at the person's specific direction.

(2) Providing general published factual information that has been written or approved by an attorney, pertaining to legal procedures, rights, or obligations to a person who is representing himself or herself in a legal matter, to assist the person in representing himself or herself. Merely publishing such factual information shall not require registration as a legal document assistant.

(3) Making published legal documents available to a person who is representing himself or herself in a legal matter.

(4) Filing and serving legal forms and documents at the specific direction of a person who is representing himself or herself in a legal matter.

(c) **A legal document assistant**, including any legal document assistant employed by a partnership or corporation, may not provide any self-help service for compensation, unless the legal document assistant is registered in the county in which his or her principal place of business is located and in any other county in which he or she performs acts for which registration is required.

Section 65. Registration: A legal document assistant shall be registered pursuant to this chapter by the county clerk in the county in which his or her principal place of business is located and in any other county in which he or she performs acts for which registration is required.

Section 66. Solicitation Requirements: (a) It is unlawful for any legal document assistant in the first in-person or telephonic solicitation of or response to a prospective client of legal document services to enter into a contract or agreement for services or accept any compensation unless the legal document assistant states orally, clearly, affirmatively and expressly all of the following, before making any other statement, except a greeting, or asking the prospective client any questions:

(1) The identity of the person making the solicitation or response to a caller.

(2) The trade name of the person represented by the person making the solicitation or response to the caller.

(3) The kind of services being offered for sale.

(4) The statement: "I am not an attorney" and, if the person offering legal document assistant services is a partnership or a corporation, or uses a fictitious business name, "(name) is not a law firm. I/we cannot represent you in court, advise you about your legal rights or the law, or select legal forms for you."

Section 67. Prohibited Acts for Legal Document Assistant: It is unlawful for any person engaged in the business or acting in the capacity of a legal document assistant to do any of the following:

(a) Provide any kind of advice, explanation, opinion, or recommendation to a consumer about possible legal rights, remedies, defenses, options, selection of forms, or strategies. A legal document assistant shall complete documents only in the manner prescribed in section 64(b).

(b) Engage in the unauthorized practice of law, including, but not limited to, giving any kind of advice, explanation, opinion, or recommendation to a consumer about possible legal rights, remedies, defenses, options, selection of forms, or strategies.

FORMAL OPINION NO. 1995-141

INTRODUCTION

This opinion addresses the ethical responsibilities of lawyers who render law-related services to a client either directly, through a non-lawyer, or through an entity in which the lawyer or the lawyer's firm has an ownership interest. "Law-related services" are services that might reasonably be performed in conjunction with and in substance are related to the provision of legal services, and that are not prohibited as unauthorized practice of law when provided by a non-lawyer.

Examples of law-related services that might be performed by a non-lawyer are such things as family counseling by a social worker, rendering tax advice by an accountant or a tax-preparer, providing financial services by a stockbroker, giving advice regarding testamentary disposition by a charity, and the like. The characteristic that such undertakings have in common is that they all present the problem that providers of such services have the opportunity to identify and refer persons using their services to lawyers, who would, of course, receive such referrals for "pecuniary gain."

Concerns frequently arise in situations where the law-related services are rendered either by an entity owned by a lawyer or a law firm, individually or with others, or by a non-lawyer employed by the lawyer or the lawyer's firm.

These practices raise ethical concerns in the areas of improper solicitation of clients and financial relationships between a lawyer and non-lawyers. This opinion addresses these concerns.

DISCUSSION

<u>Applicability of the Rules of Professional Conduct to a Lawyer's Performance of Law-Related Services</u>: Lawyers have historically been allowed to practice law and to pursue other business activities at the same time. Although the current Columbia Rules of Professional Conduct do not contain specific restrictions on dual practices, ethics opinions have warned dual practitioners that the rules place constraints on their activities in other businesses and professions.

A lawyer's ethical obligations are not limited to activities undertaken in the course of rendering pure legal services. Any act involving moral turpitude, dishonesty or corruption by an attorney, whether the act is committed in the course of the practice of law or in the pursuit of other business activities, constitutes grounds for discipline.

<u>Improper Solicitation of Clients</u>: A lawyer or law firm's performance of legal and law-related services may not involve the referral of business between the two areas of service. For example, where a lawyer offers law-related services through a person or entity in which the lawyer has an interest, whether ownership, management, or control, the lawyer may not use or encourage persons in that entity to channel or otherwise direct users of those law-related services to the lawyer if the purpose of such a practice is to attract the users as potential clients of the lawyer's law practice.

Such practices raise issues under rule 1-400, which governs lawyer solicitation. Rule 1-400 bans solicitations and prohibits in-person or telephonic communications that suggest the availability of professional services if a significant purpose of the communications is for pecuniary gain. It does not, however, bar solicitations and communications regarding the availability of purely non-legal professional services.

The ban on solicitations applies when legal employment is solicited of someone with whom the lawyer or firm does not have an existing or prior lawyer-client relationship. Thus, the rule applies when such solicitations occur in the course of rendering law-related services.

Rule 1-400 applies to solicitations and communications made on behalf of a lawyer or law firm by a non-lawyer employee or a lawyer or law firm owned, managed, or controlled entity. Thus, the rule prohibits solicitations and communications regarding the availability of legal services, which are made by a lawyer or a non-lawyer employee on behalf of the lawyer in the course of rendering law-related services.

Financial Relationships Between Lawyers and Non-Lawyers: A lawyer providing law-related services through non-lawyer employees or business entities in which non-lawyers also have an interest must also comply with the Columbia Rules of Professional Conduct governing the financial relationships between lawyers and non-lawyers. First, a lawyer shall not form a partnership with a person who is not a lawyer if any of the activities of that partnership consist of the practice of law.

Second, non-lawyers cannot share in the profits of a law practice. Rule 1-320 prevents a lawyer from directly or indirectly sharing legal fees with a non-lawyer.

Together, these rules require that both the structure of the business relationship and the division of income from law-related services be separate and distinct from the lawyer's law practice. The entity owned by the lawyer and non-lawyer cannot engage in the practice of law. The two cannot share the legal fees from the lawyer's practice.

Another area of concern is where a non-lawyer in a business relationship with a lawyer to provide law-related services seeks to influence the conduct of a lawyer's legal practice through the referral of business or imposing other profit-related concerns on the legal practice. A lawyer cannot compensate, give, or promise anything of value to any person or entity for the purpose of recommending or securing employment of the lawyer or the lawyer's firm by a client under the rule. The rule encompasses situations in which a lawyer gives any financial benefit or compensation in exchange for the referral of business.

CONCLUSION

As the preceding discussion demonstrates, the rendering of non-legal services by lawyers, law firms or entities in which either has an ownership interest raises a number of ethical concerns that must be carefully evaluated. Lawyers engaged in rendering such services must not only be aware of the ethical issues raised in this opinion, but must also watch for other ethical issues that may arise in the course of providing the service.

MEMORANDUM

TO: Roger Arbuckle

FROM: Applicant

DATE: February 28, 2012

SUBJECT: Law Offices of Richard Swayne — Business Plan

PART I.

Pursuant to the Columbia Rules of Professional Conduct (CRPC) and the Professions Code (PC), specific ethical problems relating [to] the following parts of the Business Plan are as follows:

Issue No. 1: Duties of the "receptionist" listed in the "helpline" service section of the plan.

The Free "Helpline" Service section of the Business Plan provides for the duties of the receptionist, which includes the following:

- The receptionist will answer telephones and greet customers of SHLEP.
- The receptionist will take all "helpline" calls and assist the callers in filling out the forms by answering their questions, telling them which boxes to check, and helping to formulate language to be inserted in various parts of the forms.
- The receptionist will respond to all email inquiries received from users of the forms.
- The receptionist shall also screen all callers and make an initial determination whether the caller needs legal assistance beyond mere help in filling out the forms. If so, the receptionist shall so inform the caller and tell the caller that Mr.

Swayne is available for immediate consultation for $250. If the caller agrees to pay for a consultation, the receptionist shall transfer the call to Mr. Swayne.

- The receptionist shall maintain records of the names, addresses, and telephone numbers of all "helpline" callers and, monthly, shall furnish said records to The Law Offices of Richard Swayne as "leads" Mr. Swayne may wish to pursue for client development purposes.

See Business Plan, Method of Operation, Free "Helpline" Service. However, each of the duties denotes a potential ethical problem as provided by the CRPC and PC. An analysis of each duty provided by the Business Plan is further provided below.

Answering telephones and greeting customers of SHLEP.

A receptionist is generally required to answer telephones and greet customers. As such, there are no ethical problems that can be seen at this time, relating to this particular duty.

Taking "helpline" calls and assisting callers in filling out the forms (i.e., answering questions, telling them which boxes to check, and helping to formulate language to be inserted in various parts of the forms.

Having a receptionist provide assistance to callers in filling out forms, including answering questions, telling them which boxes to check, and helping to formulate language to be inserted in various parts of the forms is an ethical violation. Specifically, as a lawyer, Swayne should not aid a person or entity in the unauthorized practice of law. CRPC, Rule 1-300. By allowing the receptionist to provide assistance to callers by the specifically stated means, Swayne is essentially allowing the receptionist to provide legal services to the callers. In fact, Swayne is aware that providing callers with what language to use is providing legal advice. See Swayne Interview Transcript, 6:22-25. As such, this duty is an ethical problem, and may be seen as the assisting [of] a non-lawyer in the unauthorized practice of law.

Responding to all email inquiries received from users of the forms.

A receptionist may have a duty in responding to all email inquiries received from users of the forms. However, it would depend on what question the user of the form has in determining whether the receptionist is providing legal services, which would be an ethical problem. As such, this duty may have an ethical problem and should be drafted to be more specific as to the types of emails the receptionist may or may not respond to, and/or how to respond to the emails if legal advice/services are requested.

Screening all callers and make an initial determination whether the caller needs legal assistance beyond mere help in filling out the forms.

Having the receptionist screen all calls and make an initial determination whether the caller needs legal assistance does not necessarily cause an ethical concern; however, if the receptionist determines that the caller does need legal assistance, having he/she tell the caller that Mr. Swayne is available for immediate consultation for $250 and then transferring the call to Swayne if the caller agrees may be an ethical problem.

CRPC Rule 1-400 states in pertinent part, "[a] solicitation shall not be made . . . on behalf of a lawyer or law firm to a prospective client with whom the lawyer or law firm has no family or prior professional relationship . . ." Specifically, a lawyer or law firm's performance of legal and law-related services may not involve the referral of business between the two areas of service. See Formal Op. No. 1995-141, Improper Solicitation of Clients. The example the Formal Opinion provides is exactly on point: "where a lawyer offers law-related services through a person or entity in which the lawyer has an interest . . . the lawyer may not use or encourage persons in that entity to channel or otherwise direct users of those law-related services to the lawyer if the purpose of such a practice is to attract the users as potential clients of the lawyer's law practice."
Here, Swayne is a limited partner of SHLEP, and has an interest in the LLP. By having the receptionist inform the caller that Swayne is available for immediate consultation in his individual capacity as a lawyer and not to answer questions relating to law-related services, where he would receive separate compensation in the amount of $250, this

will likely be considered to be improper solicitation, in violation of CRPC Rule 1-400. Formal Op.1995-141. As a result, this receptionist duty is an ethical concern and is improper solicitation.

Maintaining records of the names, addresses, and telephone numbers of all "helpline" callers.

Similar to the last duty, maintaining records of the names, addresses, and telephone numbers of all "helpline" callers may not raise any ethical concerns as it may be a duty of a receptionist to keep a client list; however, requiring her to furnished [sic] the records on a monthly basis to The Law Offices of Richard Swayne as "leads" Mr. Swayne may wish to pursue for client development purposes is an ethical concern. Specifically, CRPC Rule 1-400 bans solitications and prohibits in-person or telephonic communications that suggest the availability of professional services if a significant purpose of the communications is for pecuniary gain. Formal Op. 1995-141. The ban on solicitations applies when legal employment is solicited of someone with whom the lawyer/firm does not have an existing or prior lawyer-client relationship. Accordingly, since SHLEP is providing non-legal services, there is no lawyer-client relationship between Swayne and SHLEP's clients. Id.

Furthermore, this duty potentially may violate CPC, Section 52, if any of SHLEP's clients are in the state prisons, county jails, city jails, city prisons, or other places of detention of persons, city receiving hospitals, city and county receiving hospitals, county hospitals, superior courts, or in any public institution or in any public place or upon any public street or highway.

As such, it would be unethical for him to contact SHLEP clients to determine whether they wish to also be his law firm's clients, and allowing the receptionist to provide him with a client record to do this is an ethical concern.

<u>Issue No. 2</u>: The revenue sharing arrangements described in the plan.

The Business Plan further provides a specific provision titled "Books of Account and Sharing of Revenues". Specifically, with regard to "Sharing of Revenue", the Business Plan states as follows:

SHLEP and The Law Offices of Richard Swayne shall pay equally all costs of utilities, telephone and high-speed internet services.

SHLEP shall pay Richard Swayne from the revenues of SHLEP the agreed-upon lease rental for the office facilities on Center Street.

Mr. Swayne shall remit to SHLEP 50% of all consultation fees he receives from callers referred to him by the receptionist.

The Law Offices of Richard Swayne shall remit to SHLEP 10% of all fees earned from "leads" obtained from the receptionist.

Mr. Swayne shall reimburse one-half of the cost of health insurance and other fringe benefits provided to the receptionist.

The revenue sharing arrangement is likely to be an ethical concern. Swayne, being a lawyer providing law-related services through non-lawyer employees/business entities in which non-lawyers also have an interest must comply with the CRPC. Formal Op. 1995-141. Rule 1-320 prevents a lawyer from directly or indirectly sharing legal fees with a non-lawyer. Accordingly, by providing that Swayne will remit to SHLEP 50% of consultation fees, and 10% of all fees earned from "leads" - Rule 1-320 is in violation. Ann has 50% of SHLEP. As such, she would receive a portion of those fee percentages for the referrals provided to Swayne. Also, a lawyer cannot compensate, give, or promise anything of value to any entity for the purpose of recommending or securing employment of the lawyer/law firm by a client under this rule. Rule 1-320 also encompasses situation[s] in which a lawyer gives any financial benefit or compensation in exchange for the referral of business. To that end, the revenue sharing arrangements described in the plan may be in violation of CRPC Rule 1-320.

<u>Issue No. 3:</u> The partnership nature of the venture.

The Business Plan is contemplating the creation of a limited liability partnership (SHLEP), with the following partners:

General Partner: Ann Mouton - non-lawyer

Limited Partner: Richard Swayne - lawyer

Office Facilities: Renting out the west wing of the building where the current Law Offices of Richard Swayne are located. The rental amount is to be determined and paid to Mr. Swayne, who is the owner of the building.

Rule 1-310 states that "[a] lawyer shall not form a partnership with a person who is not a lawyer if any of the activities of that partnership consists in the practice of law." Here, Ann is a non-lawyer. Although Swayne would argue that SHLEP does not partake in the practice of law, there are aspects of SHLEP as seen in the Business Plan that indicate participation in the practice of law. For instance, the Business Plan provides that the receptionist would provide callers language to put in the form. This could be seen as providing legal advice. Furthermore, consultations with Swayne may be seen as providing legal advice. The callers would be unaware as to whether he was contacting them in his capacity as a partner of SHLEP or in his capacity as a lawyer. As such, the partnership nature of the venture is likely to be in violation of Rule 1-310, unless the Business Plan is revised to clarify that no legal services will be rendered by SHLEP.

PART II.

<u>Issue No. 4</u>: Whether Swayne's drafting the forms and instructions constitute "law-related services" and, if so, what Swayne's ethical obligations are to the users of the forms.

Law-Related Services Analysis.

As provided by the Business Plan, Production of Legal Forms section, Mr. Swayne will be responsible for determining the types of forms that are necessary and the design therefore to ensure compliance with the rules of the courts of the State of Columbia. He will also be responsible for drafting instructions for use and purposes of the forms in any advertising and marketing media utilized by SHLEP. *See* Business Plan, Production of Legal Forms (emphasis added).

Pursuant to CRPC, Rule 1-600, "law-related services" denotes services that might reasonably be performed in conjunction with and in substance are related to the provision of legal service and that are not prohibited as unauthorized practice of law when provided by a non-lawyer. Moreover, the CPC, Section 25 provides that the practice of law is the provision of legal services and includes, but is not limited to, giving any kind of advice, explanation, opinion, or recommendation to a consumer about possible legal rights, remedies, defenses, options, selection of forms, or strategy.

Accordingly, even though Mr. Swayne is responsible for designing the forms to be in compliance with the state rules, he is also responsible for drafting instructions for use and drafting the purposes of the forms in advertising and marketing media. In essence, one could argue that he is providing an explanation and/or recommendation to consumers about their possible legal rights and/or selection of forms, which may constitute legal services. However, if a non-lawyer is able to draft forms and instructions, then those responsibilities will constitute as "law-related services".

Formal Opinion No. 1995-141 provides examples of law-related services that may be performed by non-lawyers including family counseling by a social worker, rendering tax advice by an accountant or a tax-preparer, providing financial services by a stockbroker, and giving advice regarding testamentary disposition by a charity. See Formal Op. No. 1995-141, Introduction. The characteristic that each example has in common is that the undertakings all present the problem that providers of such services have the opportunity to identify and refer persons using their services to lawyers, who would, of course, receive such referrals for "pecuniary gain". *Id.*

30

Here, Swayne's drafting of forms and instructions allows the consumer to determine what form he/she needs by reading the instructions relating to the use and purposes of the forms that he drafted. If the consumer has any questions and contacts the helpline, the receptionist should refer the consumer to a lawyer, Mr. Swayne. To that end, it is likely that drafting of the forms and instructions will constitute "law-related services".

Swayne's Ethical Obligation to the Users of the Forms.

Nonetheless, even if drafting of the forms and instructions constitute "law-related services", Rule 1-600 further applies to the provision of law-related services by a lawyer even when the lawyer does not provide any legal services to the person for whom the law-related services are performed regardless of whether the law-related services are performed through a law firm or separate entity. CRPC, Rule 1-600, Discussion.

Since Mr. Swayne, in his capacity of limited partner for SHLEP, will be drafting the forms and instructions (i.e., law-related services), and because he is a lawyer, it is irrelevant whether he provides any legal services to a SHLEP caller. Mr. Swayne's conduct involved in the provision of law-related services is subject to the Rules that apply generally to lawyer conduct, regardless of whether the conduct involves the provision of legal services. CRPC, Rule 1-600, Discussion.

Accordingly, Mr. Swayne would need to take reasonable measures to assure that each person using SHLEP's services that the services provided are not legal services and that the Rules of Professional Conduct that relate to the client-lawyer relationship do not apply. *Id.* Furthermore, regardless of the sophistication of potential recipients of law-related services, Mr. Swayne will need to take special care to keep the separate provision of law-related services and legal services in order to minimize the risk that the recipient will assume that the law related-services are legal services. *Id.* Mr. Swayne must take reasonable measures to communicate a clear, understandable disclaimer to assure that the recipient of the law-related services knows that the services are not legal services and the protections of the client-lawyer relationship do not apply. *Id.*

<u>Issue No. 5</u>: What obligation, if any, Swayne might have to supervise the "receptionist".

As previously discussed, the responsibilities of the receptionist, as outlined above, encompass more than simply receptionist duties and responsibilities. Specifically, the receptionist for SHLEP is not only required to answer telephones and greet customers of SHLEP, but is also required to assist callers in filling out the forms by answering their questions, telling them which boxes to check, and helping to formulate language to be inserted in various parts of the forms, respond to all email inquiries received from users of the forms, screen all callers and make an initial determination whether the caller needs legal assistance beyond mere help in filling out the forms, inform the caller that Mr. Swayne is available for immediate consultation for $250, and maintain records of the names, addresses, and telephone numbers of all "helpline" callers and, monthly, shall furnish said records to The Law Offices of Richard Swayne as "leads" Mr. Swayne may wish to pursue for client development purposes.

Furthermore, Mr. Swayne himself believes that the receptionist would also direct clients of his who come in for appointments or consultations with him. See Swayne Interview, 5:22-23. Accordingly, the "receptionist" for SHLEP would also be working for Mr. Swayne in his capacity as a lawyer of The Law Offices of Richard Swayne, and therefore, Mr. Swayne has an obligation to supervise the receptionist pursuant to CRPC, Rule 1-500.

Mr. Swayne will need to provide the receptionist with appropriate instruction and supervision concerning the ethical aspects of their employment, particularly regarding the obligation not to disclose information relating to the representation of the client, and should be responsible for their work product. See CRPC, Rule 1-500, Discussion. He will need to provide for measures, taking into account that the receptionist does not have legal training and is not subject to professional discipline. This is especially relevant since the receptionist speaks to all helpline callers and maintains records of the names, addresses, and telephone numbers of all helpline callers.

Furthermore, the receptionist is contemplated with being provided with the responsibility of assisting callers [to] fill out forms, telling them which boxes to check, and helping them formulate language to be inserted in various parts of the forms. Thus, Mr. Swayne has an obligation to provide the receptionist with appropriate instruction and supervision in ensuring that he/she does not provide legal advice.

To: Roger Arbuckle

From: Applicant

Date: 2/28/12

RE: Law Offices of Richard Swayne - Business Plan

You have asked me to draft a two-part memorandum preparing you for your upcoming meeting with our client, Richard Swayne ("RS"). RS has provided us with a business plan (the "Plan") that calls for him to join forces with an old college roommate of his, Ann Moulton ("AM"), in a limited liability partnership called Self-Help Legal Enterprise Project, LLP ("SHLEP"). SHLEP's Plan, as well as RS's existing legal practice as a solo practitioner, raises a number of ethical concerns that you asked me to research.

Part 1 of this memorandum deals with the specific ethical problems that certain parts of the Plan present under the Columbia Rules of Professional Conduct ("Rules") and the Columbia Professions Code ("Code"). As well, reference is made to the State Bar of Columbia Standing Committee on Professional Responsibility and Conduct Formal Opinion No. 1995-141 (the "Opinion"). Part 2 outlines whether Swayne's activities under the Plan are law-related services, if so, whether he has any ethical obligations to customers of SHLEP, and finally whether he has any obligations to supervise the receptionist that SHLEP will hire under the Plan.

Part I: Ethical Problems Created by the Plan

Subpart (A): Ethical Issues Regarding the Duties of the Receptionist Listed in the Helpline Service Section of the Plan

The Plan calls for the receptionist to engage in a number of tasks while operating "free Helpline services", including:

(1) Answering telephones and greeting SHLEP's customers;

(2) Assisting callers in filling out legal forms by answering questions, telling them which boxes to check, and helping formulate language to be inserted into various parts of the forms;

(3) Responding to email inquiries;

(4) Screening callers and making an initial determination whether the caller needs legal assistance; if so, informing the caller that RS is available for a $250 fee, and transferring the caller to RS if he or she agrees to pay the fee; and

(5) Maintaining records of each caller's address, name, and telephone number, and monthly furnishing all of said information to RS's legal practice as "leads" for him to pursue via client development.

Each of these implicates grave ethical concerns under both the Code and the Rules, as well as the Opinion, all of which are analyzed more fully below.

Unauthorized Practice of Law

Rule 1-300 proscribes any attorney from aiding any person or entity in the unauthorized practice of law. Code Section 25 defines the practice of law as giving any kind of advice, explanation, opinion, or recommendation to a consumer about possible legal rights, remedies, defenses, options, selection of forms, or strategies. Further, Code Section 67(b) provides that it is illegal for a legal document assistant to engage in the unauthorized practice of law, including ". . . giving any kind of advice . . . to a consumer about . . . selection of forms or strategies."

Arguably, the receptionist is engaged in the unauthorized practice of law in violation of Code Sections 25 and 67(b), and thus RS is aiding him or her in the unauthorized practice of law in violation of Rule 1-300. The receptionist is responsible for answering questions from callers about which boxes to check, and formulating language to be inserted into the various legal forms. The receptionist is also making the initial determination of whether a caller needs legal help. This is likely giving advice about the selection of forms under Code Section 67(b), and thus the receptionist would need to be licensed pursuant to Code Section 25. Furthermore, as a partner of SHLEP and acquiescing to the Plan, RS is thus aiding the receptionist in the acts called for by the Helpline Services. Thus, you should advise RS that any discretionary decision-making by the receptionist in terms of the forms selected or the language inserted into such forms is the unauthorized practice of law, and thus a violation of the Code and the Rules.

Impermissible Solicitation

Rule 1-400 proscribes any solicitation "made by or on behalf of a lawyer . . . to a prospective client with whom the lawyer or the law firm has no family or prior professional relationship" unless otherwise protected by Columbia law. Under the rule, solicitation is "any communication concerning availability for professional employment of a lawyer. . . in which a significant motive is pecuniary gain and that is delivered in person or by telephone." Furthermore, the Opinion states that a "lawyer may not use or encourage persons in [a non-legal] entity to channel or otherwise direct users of those law-related services to the lawyer if the purpose of such a practice is to attract the users as potential clients of the lawyer's law practice."

Here, the Plan calls for the receptionist to make impermissible solicitations. First, the Plan requires the receptionist to inform callers that RS is available for a $250 fee, and transfer the caller to RS if he or she agrees to pay that fee. This is a solicitation under Rule 1-400 because it is made on behalf of RS (he pays half of the receptionist's salary and the arrangement is detailed in the Plan), and there is [sic] no facts showing a prior business or family relationship with SHLEP's customers. Furthermore, the motive is pecuniary gain under 1-400 because RS wants clients for business development and it is delivered over the telephone by the receptionist. Thus, the receptionist is making a solicitation for SHLEP to direct services to RS's law practice in contravention of the Opinion's proscription of the same. You should advise RS that the receptionist may not divert business to his legal practice under the Code, the Rules, and the Opinion.

Registration as a Legal Document Assistant

Code Sections 64(c) and 65 provide that a legal document assistant may not provide any self-help service for compensation unless he or she is registered with the county in which the help is given. A legal document assistant under Section 64(a) is any person . . . that provides . . . , for compensation, any self-help service to a member of the public who is representing himself in a legal matter." However, "merely secretarial or receptionist services" do not qualify, as provided by Section 64(b).

Here, the receptionist is arguably a legal document assistant under the Code, and thus must register with the County before engaging in such services. Although 64(a) provides an exemption for purely secretarial or receptionist services, 64(b) defines a self-help service as completing legal documents in a ministerial manner or providing general published factual information that has been written or approved by an attorney, to a person who is representing himself or herself. Under the Plan, the receptionist must assist callers in filling out forms by answering questions, telling them which boxes to check, and helping them formulate language to be inserted into the parts of the forms. Although it's not clear whether the receptionist may fill out the forms himself or herself, the likely act of telling the customers which box to check qualifies as "completing legal documents in a ministerial manner." This is a self-help service. Furthermore, it is done for consideration, as the customer pays for the right to use the form and receive help. Finally, as called for by the Plan, the customer is representing himself or herself in a legal matter, and thus the elements of Section 64 and 65 are met. You should advise RS that the receptionist needs to register under Code Section 65 as a legal document assistant in the county in which the office is located and any other counties where SHLEP may do business.

Disclaimer on All Solicitation from a Legal Document Assistant

Code Section 66 requires a legal document assistant, during telephonic solicitation, to make an oral, clear, affirmative, and express disclaimer with the following information: his or her identity, the trade name of the business he or she represents, the kind of services offered for sale, the statement that he or she is not an attorney, and that there is no attorney-client relationship from the services.

Here, the receptionist is likely in violation of Section 66. The Plan's duties under the Helpline Service do not require any disclaimer that there is no attorney-client relationship, and further does not require any statement that he or she is not an attorney. As argued above, the receptionist is also a legal document assistant, qualifying for treatment under Section 66. Thus, the receptionist is in violation of Section 66's disclaimer requirements. Accordingly, you should advise RS that he needs to have the receptionist read off the proper disclaimer under Section 66, including a statement that he or she is not an attorney and that there exists no attorney-client relationship.

Impermissible Fee Sharing and/or Payments to the Receptionist for "Leads" that Act as Referrals

Rule 1-320 prohibits a lawyer from compensating "any person . . . for the purpose of recommending or securing employment of the lawyer . . . or as a reward for having made a recommendation resulting in employment of the lawyer." Furthermore, the Opinion affirms that a "lawyer cannot compensate . . . any person . . . for the purpose of recommending or securing" a lawyer under Rule 1-320.

Here, the receptionist is likely in violation of Rule 1-320. RS reimburses one-half of the cost of health insurance and fringe benefits for the receptionist, as well as remitting 50% of all consultation fees and 10% of all fees from leads that the Plan calls for the receptionist to forward to RS on a monthly basis. Thus, he is compensating the receptionist, albeit indirectly, as a reward for having recommending [sic] clients to his law practice. More directly, the receptionist also forwards callers to RS's legal office provided they agree to pay his $250 consultation fee. This is impermissible payment for referrals under Rule 1-320, and you should advise RS that he may not pay any compensation to the receptionist, nor reimburse SHLEP for referral fees from the receptionist's work.

Subpart (B): Ethical Issues Regarding the Plan's Revenue Sharing Arrangements

Rule 1-320 proscribes a lawyer from "directly or indirectly shar[ing] legal fees with a person who is not a lawyer." The Opinion affirms this rule by stating that "non-lawyers cannot share in the profits of a law practice."

Here, however, the Plan's terms call for a violation of Rule 1-320 and the Opinion. The Plan suggests that RS shall pay SHLEP 50% of his consultation fees from callers referred by the receptionist, as well as 10% of the leads. This is directly sharing legal fees with a person, AM, who is not a lawyer. RS recognizes that these fees are necessary because SHLEP would "refer a lot" of customers to RS's practice and also provide "client leads". Thus, he would need to "share with the LLP some of the referral fees." Although RS's law practice and SHLEP will keep separate financial records and books, the sharing of this percentage of his fees is enough to run afoul of Rule 1-320 and the Opinion. Thus, you should advise RS that the fee sharing arrangements are a violation of the Rules and the Code.

Subpart (C): Ethical Issues Regarding the Partnership Nature of the Venture

Rule 1-310 prohibits a lawyer from forming "a partnership with a person who is not a lawyer if any of the activities that the partnership consists of the practice of law." The Opinion affirms the same. Furthermore, sections of the Code and Rules, referenced above, are incorporated herein to define the practice of law.

The partnership agreement likely runs afoul of Rule 1-310. Here, as discussed above, the receptionist's activities of advising customers what blanks to fill in and what boxes to check are likely the practice of law. Additionally, RS's own interview showed that he will have a role in creating the forms and instructions for use of the forms, cindlugin [sic] what forms to use for specific purposes. In fact, the Plan calls for the website to advertise that the forms were created by RS, an experienced attorney in Columbia. This is the practice of law, and as a component of SHLEP's services, it means that RS and AM formed a partnership where at least some activities are the practice of law.

Because AM is not an attorney and RS is an attorney, the partnership is in violation of Rule 1-310. You should advise RS that the partnership is not permissible under the Rules.

Part II: Swayne's Activities as Law-Related Services, His Ethical Obligations to Customers of SHLEP, and His Duties to Supervise the Receptionist

Subpart (A): Whether Swayne's Drafting of the Forms and Instructions Constitute Law-Related Services

Rule 1-600 defines law-related services as those "that might reasonably be performed in conjunction with and in substance are related to the provision of legal services, and that are not prohibited as unauthorized practice of law when provided by a non-lawyer." The comments to the Rules suggest that a lawyer may be providing law-related services even when he or she does so through an entity that is not a law firm. The Opinion further clarifies that law-related services may include, by way of example, family counseling, tax advice, financial services, or advising on a testamentary disposition by a charity. Those situations encumber "the opportunity to identify and refer persons" to closely-related lawyer, who could gain financially from such referrals.

Arguably, RS is involved in something beyond merely providing law-related services. Rule 1-600 seems to suggest that law-related services are merely ancillary to the actual practice of law, and the key facet of the rule is that law-related services would not be prohibited as the unauthorized practice of law if done by a non-lawyer. The Opinion's examples solidify this. Family counseling is the usual province of a family therapist, tax advice of an accountant, and financial services of a financial investment specialist. Here, however, RS admitted in his interview that he would provide limited free consultations over the phone, including answering simple questions for free. Furthermore, he would create pleading forms such as summons, complaints, answers, discovery documents, motions, and the like. Furthermore, he would draft instructions on what forms to use for SPECIFIC purposes. The Plan also emphasizes RS's role in the forms, and the website provides various descriptions of forms and their uses and filing instructions. Any of these would likely be the practice of law (i.e. Code Section 25 suggests the practice of law includes giving advice about "selection of forms" to use in litigation) if done by a non-lawyer, an[d] all activities are the province not of non-lawyers, but of existing lawyers. Thus, it is unlikely that RS is performing law-related services; instead he is likely practicing law by performing his role under the Plan.

Subpart (B): RS's Ethical Obligations to SHLEP Customers If He is Providing Law-Related Services

By way of a complete analysis, assuming that RS is performing law-related services, he has certain ethical obligations to SHLEP's customers under the Rules, the Code, and the Opinion. Rule 1-600(B) provides that a lawyer will be liable under the Code if the law-related services are provided by the lawyer in circumstances that are not distinct from the lawyer's provision of legal services to the client; or if the services are provided by an entity controlled by the lawyer, he or she fails to take reasonable measures to ensure that the person obtaining the law-related services knows that the services are not legal services and the attorney-client privilege does not exist for those services.

The Rule's comments further add that regardless of the customer's sophistication, the lawyer should take special care to separate the legal services from those that are merely law-related services, which an attorney satisfies by taking "reasonable measures to communicate a clear, understandable disclaimer to assure that the customer of law-related services knows that they are not legal services and that the protections of the attorney-client relationship do not exist."

Here, RS will be subject to the Rules for these law-related services on either prong of 1-600(B). As to the first prong, the circumstances of his services are not distinct from his provision of legal services. First, his law practice and SHLEP share the same building. Second, SHLEP's website indicates that the forms are specifically provided by RS and list his credentials as an attorney. Third, the receptionist transfers all callers that are interested in RS's services to his law office for a consultation, including an agreement up-front about his consultation fee. Although RS did admit in his interview that he has his own phone number for the law office, nor does he think he has any control over the

41

receptionist, the Plan and SHLEP's website to [sic] not "distinctly" separate RS's role in SHLEP from his law practice. Thus, under the first prong, he must comply with Rule 1-600.

Even assuming he does not qualify for treatment under the first prong, he does control an entity, SHLEP, under the second prong and there do not appear to be any reasonable measures to assure that customer knows that he or she is not receiving legal advice and that no attorney-client relationship exists. First, RS owns 50% of SHLEP, and he shares equally in the profit and losses. Second, he pays the fringe benefits and health insurance of the receptionist, suggesting that he has control over the entity. Second, there are no reasonable measures on our facts. Neither the website nor the receptionist warns that there is no attorney-client relationship or that the services are not legal services. Accordingly, RS fails under the terms of Rule 1-600 for law-related services, and thus you should advise that he needs to include a clear disclaimer that he is not providing legal services for SHLEP and that there is no attorney-client relationship for customers of SHLEP.

Subpart (C): RS's Obligations to Supervise the Receptionist

Rule 1-500 provides that a lawyer having direct supervisory authority over the non-lawyer shall make reasonable efforts to ensure that the person's conduct is compatible with the professional obligations of the lawyer. The comments to Rule 1-500 note that a lawyer must give assistants appropriate instruction and supervision concerning the ethical aspects of their employment, particularly regarding the obligation not to disclose information relating to the representation of the client, and should be responsible for their work product. The Opinion further notes that Rule 1-400 applies to solicitations and communications made on behalf of a lawyer or law firm by a non-lawyer employee or a lawyer or law-firm owned, managed, or controlled entity.

Here, it is a close call whether RS has any obligations to supervise the receptionist; however, because ethical concerns are involved and the Opinion warns that "rules place constraints on [dual practictioners] activities in other businesses and professions," the best view is that RS does have ethical obligations to supervise the receptionist. First, RS, in his interview, argued that he would not have any supervisory role or authority over the receptionist. He suggested AM "alone would be supervising the receptionist." This suggests that he does not have any "direct supervisory authority" over the receptionist. However, he also noted that he would own 50% of SHLEP, and that the receptionist's duties would be to direct clients who come in for appointments or consultations to his office. Furthermore, if a person had a question for RS, he admitted that the receptionist would "direct that person" to him as well. The Plan's terms also provide that RS will pay for one-half of the receptionist's fringe benefits and health insurance, and that he or she will maintain records of SHLEP customers and provide them each month to RS's law practice for further client development. Also, the Plan notes that SHLEP would be hiring the receptionist, and that RS would contribute $100,000 in start-up money to SHLEP to help start the business. Finally, although RS is a limited partner in SHLEP, much of the partnership activity is designed to funnel money to RS's law practice, as he admitted in his interview. On the sum of these facts, RS likely has some supervisory authority over the receptionist, and thus he has an obligation under Rule 1-500 to give him or her appropriate instruction and supervision concerning the ethical aspects on the employment.

Conclusion

The Plan, as drafted and as described by RS during his interview, likely violates a number of provisions under the Code and the Rules, as well as running afoul of the Opinion. Furthermore, SHLEP likely requires RS to take on additional supervisory duties over the receptionist, as well as the business activities of SHLEP. You should give a strong warning to RS about these matters, and encourage him to revise the Plan accordingly to stay on the proper side of his ethical obligations as an attorney. And of course, should he wish to revise the Plan, our services are available to him to achieve ethical compliance with the Code and Rules while still entertaining his novel business opportunity.

Performance Test B
INSTRUCTIONS AND FILE

STATE v. DOLAN

STATE v. DOLAN
INSTRUCTIONS

1. This performance test is designed to evaluate your ability to handle a select number of legal authorities in the context of a factual problem involving a client.

2. The problem is set in the fictional State of Columbia, one of the United States.

3. You will have two sets of materials with which to work: a File and a Library.

4. The File contains factual materials about your case. The first document is a memorandum containing the instructions for the tasks you are to complete.

5. The Library contains the legal authorities needed to complete the tasks. The case reports may be real, modified, or written solely for the purpose of this performance test. If the cases appear familiar to you, do not assume that they are precisely the same as you have read before. Read each thoroughly, as if it were new to you. You should assume that cases were decided in the jurisdictions and on the dates shown. In citing cases from the Library, you may use abbreviations and omit page citations.

6. You should concentrate on the materials provided, but you should also bring to bear on the problem your general knowledge of the law. What you have learned in law school and elsewhere provides the general background for analyzing the problem; the File and Library provide the specific materials with which you must work.

7. Although there are no restrictions on how you apportion your time, you should probably allocate at least 90 minutes to reading and organizing before you begin preparing your response.

8. Your response will be graded on its compliance with instructions and on its content, thoroughness, and organization.

Richard Parsons
State's Attorney

Date: March 1, 2012

To: Applicant
From: Richard Parsons
Re: State v. Dolan

As you may know, this office is prosecuting Bruce Dolan. Mr. Dolan is charged with 1) possession of methamphetamine and marijuana, 2) possession with intent to distribute methamphetamine and marijuana, and 3) conspiracy to distribute methamphetamine and marijuana.

The nonjury bench trial was completed yesterday and closing arguments were scheduled for this morning. Unfortunately, Barbara Jordan, the Assistant State's Attorney trying the case, has gone into the hospital for an emergency appendectomy. The court has given us an extension of time until tomorrow to present closing arguments. I will present the closing argument, but I want you to prepare a draft of that closing argument for my review.

Please write out the argument exactly as you would give it if you were presenting it. It might be helpful to read the Library first. You need to understand the elements of each charge in order to understand how each witness' testimony establishes the facts necessary to support our argument that each of the elements has been proven beyond a reasonable doubt.

Follow the guidelines contained in the office memo on Closing Arguments: Bench Trials.

Richard Parsons
State's Attorney

Date: September 1, 2011

To: Assistant State's Attorneys
From: Richard Parsons
Re: Closing Arguments: Bench Trials

Your closing argument should begin with an understanding of the elements of the crime that will be applied to the facts in the case. In jury trials, you will have jury instructions. In bench trials, however, you must rely on your analysis of legal authority (statutes and case law) during closing argument. The legal authorities in bench trials (just as the instructions in jury trials) will give you the framework for your closing argument. The argument must show how the evidence admitted during the trial meets the required elements established by the statutes and case law. While in a jury trial you do not ordinarily discuss or make reference to the legal authorities, in a bench trial you have more latitude in referring to the legal authority. Indeed, in the absence of jury instructions, you may find it necessary to explain to the court finer points of the law. But, you must not lose sight of the fact that a closing argument is not a legal memo or an essay. The argument is based on the evidence presented, not histrionics or personal opinion.

Your job is to help the judge understand how the law relates to the facts presented, and to persuade the judge that he or she has no choice but to find as you have advocated. Do the following:

-- Address each charge separately.

-- For each charge state the elements that are required to get a conviction.

-- Argue that the evidence establishes each element beyond a reasonable doubt.

-- Draw reasonable inferences from the evidence to support your position.

-- Never hold back any argument assuming you will have a second opportunity to make it in rebuttal.

Organization and persuasiveness are very important. If you immerse the judge in a sea of unconnected details, he or she will not have a coherent point of view.

TRIAL TRANSCRIPT

STATE v. DOLAN

EXAMINATION OF RODNEY MACK

Rodney Mack, a witness called by the state, first being duly sworn, testified as follows:

DIRECT EXAMINATION BY MS. JORDAN

Q: Would you tell us your name?

A: Rodney Mack.

Q: Where do you work?

A: I am unemployed.

Q: Where do you live?

A: I am a guest of the county, at the jail.

Q: What were you arrested for?

A: Possession of controlled substances.

Q: Drugs?

A: Yes.

. . .

Q: Are you familiar with the defendant Bruce Dolan?

A: We went to high school together and we did a little business on the side.

Q: What business?

A: Dolly would sell me drugs that I would then resell.

Q: By Dolly you mean the defendant.

A: Yeah; all his friends called him by the nickname "Dolly."

Q: What was the time frame during which you had this relationship?

A: Must have been basically June 2008 through September or October 2010.

Q: Were you the only person the defendant supplied?

A: No; he sold to a close-knit group of friends and neighbors.

Q: Who?

A: Me, Lynette Rogers, Will Gardner, Tom Cord.

Q: Did these people have anything in common other than buying drugs?

A: Actually we all went to high school together and some are related in one way or another.

1   **Q:** What exactly are the family relations?

2   **A:** My daughter married and had a child with Lynette Rogers' son.

3   **Q:** What type of drugs would you purchase?

4   **A:** Methamphetamine and marijuana.

5   **Q:** Did the defendant ever tell you where he obtained the drugs he sold to you?

6   **A:** He never actually said; he only told me that he got the drugs, buried and stored them

7   on his property, and had friends come to his property to obtain and use drugs.

8   **Q:** Was this a rural setting?

9   **A:** He lived in rural Montour, Columbia, along the Columbia River, in a one room shack,

10   on property that used to be a Boy Scout camp.

11   **Q:** Other than his friends, did he sell the drugs directly to users?

12   **A:** He told me he used his friends to actually distribute the drugs.

13   **Q:** Specifically, what drugs did you buy from the defendant?

14   **A:** Meth.

15   **Q:** How much did you buy?

16   **A:** One-quarter pound at a time.

17   **Q:** Where did you buy the drugs?

18   **A:** He had really strict rules. A couple of us could buy at his house, but others would

19   have to meet him in Tama and the casino.

20   **Q:** Where did *you* buy?

21   **A:** It really depended. Both places really.

22   **Q:** What types of arrangements were made about the price?

23   **A:** Again, he was very rigid; cash only, nothing larger than $20 bills. No negotiation on

24   price. Strictly take it or leave it.

25   **Q:** What did you do with the drugs?

26   **A:** I sold the drugs to others in the Kellogg and Newton, Columbia areas.

27   **Q:** Who did you sell it to?

28   **A:** I broke it into ounces to sell to at least four people. Richard Crutchfield. I can't

29   remember who the others were.

30   . . .

31

32

Q: You have been charged with possession of meth with intent to distribute, haven't you?

A: Yes.

Q: In fact, haven't you cut a deal with the prosecutor in this case that if you testify against Mr. Dolan, he will let you plead to a reduced crime?

A: Yes.

Q: You remain close to Mr. Dolan, don't you?

A: Not any more.

Q: Let's try this, then. Weren't you a friend of Mr. Dolan for a long time?

A: Since high school.

Q: You hung out together?

A: Yes.

Q: Drank together?

A: Some.

Q: Actually, you were arrested once together, weren't you?

BY MS. JORDAN: Objection.

BY THE COURT: Overruled.

Q: You have been convicted of a felony yourself, haven't you?

A: Yes.

Q: That was three years ago?

A: I think that's right.

Q: The conviction was for sale of narcotics, is that right?

A: I believe that's what they called it.

Q: You spent 18 months in prison, correct?

A: Yes.

Q: I assume it was unpleasant in prison.

A: Not a great experience.

Q: You don't want to go back, do you?

A: Not particularly.

. . .

EXAMINATION OF RICHARD CRUTCHFIELD

Richard Crutchfield, a witness called by the state, first being duly sworn, testified as follows:

DIRECT EXAMINATION BY MS. JORDAN

Q: Would you tell us your name?

A: Richard Crutchfield.

Q: Where do you work?

A: I am currently unemployed.

Q: Where do you live?

A: I am currently in jail.

Q: What were you arrested for?

A: Possession of meth.

. . .

Q: Have you ever purchased methamphetamine?

A: Yes.

Q: From whom?

A: From both Tom Cord and Rodney Mack. When one of them was not available, I would purchase methamphetamine from the other.

Q: Did you ever have occasion to go to the Tama casino with Mr. Mack?

A: Yeah; he and I went to the casino in Tama and Mack would leave the casino to pick up methamphetamine.

CROSS-EXAMINATION BY MS. MAYER

Q: You have been charged with possession of meth with intent to distribute, haven't you?

A: Yes.

Q: In fact, haven't you cut a deal with the prosecutor in this case that if you testify against Mr. Dolan, he will let you plead to a reduced crime?

A: Yes.

Q: You've known Mr. Dolan for almost 10 years, correct?

A: Yes.

. . .

1

2   Tom Cord, a witness called by the state, first being duly sworn, testified as follows:

3   DIRECT EXAMINATION BY MS. JORDAN

4   . . .

5   **Q:** Are you familiar with the defendant Bruce Dolan?

6   **A:** We went to high school together.

7   **Q:** Did you do any business together?

8   **A:** Yes.

9   **Q:** What business?

10 **A:** He would sell me drugs that I would then resell.

11 **Q:** What was the time frame during which you had this relationship?

12 **A:** From around June of 2009 through December of 2010.

13 **Q:** How much did you purchase during this period?

14 **A:** Maybe a couple of pounds of methamphetamine a month at most.

15 **Q:** Where did you buy the drugs?

16 **A:** Always at his house or I would have to meet him in Tama at the casino.

17 **Q:** What types of arrangements were made about the price?

18 **A:** Cash only, nothing larger than $20 bills. He would get really angry if you tried to

19 negotiate the price. He always said "take it or leave it."

20 **Q:** Are you familiar with Rodney Mack?

21 **A:** Yes. We went to high school together.

22 **Q:** Have you remained close?

23 **A:** Yes.

24 CROSS-EXAMINATION BY MS. MAYER

25 **Q:** You have been charged with possession of meth with intent to distribute, haven't

26 you?

27 **A:** Yes.

28 **Q:** In fact, haven't you cut a deal with the prosecutor in this case that if you testify

29 against Mr. Dolan, he will let you plead to a reduced crime?

30 **A:** Yes.

31

32

REDIRECT EXAMINATION BY MS. JORDAN

1

2 **Q:** You remain close to Mr. Mack, don't you?

3 **A:** Yes.

4 **Q:** When you finished a violator program in Altaville, Columbia, Rodney Mack picked

5 you up?

6 **A:** Yes.

7 **Q:** Indeed, you met your girlfriend, Stacey Carroll Black, through Rodney and Renee

8 Mack?

9 **A:** Yes.

10   <u>EXAMINATION OF LYNETTE ROGERS</u>

11 Lynette Rogers, a witness called by the state, first being duly sworn, testified as follows:

12   DIRECT EXAMINATION BY MS. JORDAN

13 . . .

14 **Q:** Did you ever buy drugs from the defendant, Bruce Dolan?

15 **A:** He would sell drugs to my brother, Will Gardner. Will would then resell the drugs.

16 **Q:** When did this take place?

17 **A:** It was around October 2009. I began taking my brother to defendant's residence to

18 obtain marijuana and methamphetamine to sell to others.

19 **Q:** If it was your brother who was buying, why did you take him?

20 **A:** Will was quadriplegic. He needed to earn some quick money for medical bills, and for

21 one month, I helped him sell controlled substances.

22 **Q:** Did you just show up at the defendant's home and ask to buy it?

23 **A:** No; I arranged by phone for Will to buy methamphetamine from defendant.

24 **Q:** Did you know the defendant before you made the call?

25 **A:** I knew the defendant through my boyfriend, Billy Purvis. Billy had gotten one-half

26 ounce to one-ounce quantities of methamphetamine from Rodney Mack and told me

27 that Rodney got it from Dolly.

28 **Q:** How much did you buy from the defendant in total?

29 **A:** Had to be somewhere between twelve to fourteen ounces of methamphetamine.

30 **Q:** Did you buy it all at once?

31 **A:** No, no. Will usually bought two ounces of methamphetamine at a time from

32 defendant, and sold most of it to Todd Bram.

1   **Q:** Where did you buy the drugs?

2   **A:** At his house, sometimes in Tama, at the casino.

3   **Q:** What types of arrangements were made about the price?

4   **A:** He would only accept $20 bills.

5   **Q:** Did you negotiate the price?

6   **A:** Absolutely not. He was very clear he would not do that.

7   **Q:** Your Honor, at this point, I ask the court to take judicial notice of the fact that

8   defendant's home phone number as published in the directory is 555-555-2345.

9   **BY THE COURT:** So noted.

10   **Q:** Showing you what has been marked as State's Exhibit 50, do you recognize it?

11   **A:** Yes.

12   **Q:** What is it?

13   **A:** It's my cell phone bill from October 19, 2009, to December 15, 2009.

14   **Q:** Does it show any calls to the defendant's phone number?

15   **A:** It shows three calls to the defendant's residence.

16   CROSS-EXAMINATION BY MS. MAYER

17   **Q:** Your brother is dead, isn't he?

18   **BY MS. JORDAN:** Objection, irrelevant.

19   **BY MS. MAYER:** Goes to bias, Your Honor.

20   **BY THE COURT:** Overruled.

21   **Q:** Again, your brother is dead, isn't he?

22   **A:** Yes.

23   **Q:** He died from an overdose of meth, is that correct?

24   **A:** Yes.

25   <u>EXAMINATION OF TODD BRAM</u>

26   Todd Bram, a witness called by the state, first being duly sworn, testified as follows:

27   DIRECT EXAMINATION BY MS. JORDAN

28   . . .

29   **Q:** Have you ever purchased meth?

30   **A:** Yes.

31

32

1 **Q:** When and from whom?

2 **A:** I purchased an ounce of methamphetamine from Will Gardner once or twice a week

3 for three to four months between October and December 2009.

4 **Q:** Where did the sales take place?

5 **A:** Usually at the casino in Tama.

6 **Q:** How did you come to identify Mr. Gardner as a source?

7 **A:** I had heard that Dolly was dealing and I approached him. Dolly told me he didn't do

8 retail, that I should check out someone like Will Gardner.

9 ....

10 <u>EXAMINATION OF STACEY BLACK</u>

11 Stacey Black, a witness called by the state, first being duly sworn, testified as follows:

12 DIRECT EXAMINATION BY MS. JORDAN

13 ....

14 **Q:** Have you ever been to the defendant's home?

15 **A:** Yes, though I have never seen him there.

16 **Q:** Why were you there?

17 **A:** I went twice, with Tom Cord.

18 **Q:** Why?

19 **A:** The first time I did not realize Tom was buying drugs. I only found out when we

20 arrived. Tom made me wait in the car.

21 **Q:** How do you know he got drugs?

22 **A:** Easy. We were driving back and Tom was arrested by the police after a traffic stop.

23 **Q:** What happened?

24 **A:** Tom's car was impounded. Tom whispered to me that the car contained an ounce of

25 marijuana and one-quarter pound of methamphetamine that he had just picked up from

26 defendant.

27 **Q:** What did you do?

28 **A:** I got the drugs while the car was impounded and returned them to Tom.

29 **Q:** If the car was impounded, how did you get the drugs?

30 **A:** Just a second set of keys. The car was just sitting there in the police station parking

31 lot.

32

Q: When was the second trip to the defendant's?

A: Sometime after the first stop.

Q: Did Tom drive?

A: No. I drove because Tom was too tweaked out to drive. Tom had been awake too long, needed sleep, and was nervous about driving back to defendant's residence after the arrest after the traffic stop.

Q: Did Tom buy drugs?

A: Yes, I saw him bring about one-quarter pound of methamphetamine and an ounce of marijuana out of the house.

. . .

CROSS-EXAMINATION BY MS. MAYER

. . .

<u>EXAMINATION OF B. J. ATWOOD</u>

B.J. Atwood, a witness called by the state, first being duly sworn, testified as follows:

DIRECT EXAMINATION BY MS. JORDAN

Q: Would you tell us your name?

A: B.J. Atwood.

Q: Where do you work?

A: I am a Detective with the Columbia Drug Enforcement Administration.

Q: How long have you worked with the CDEA?

A: Fifteen years.

Q: Do you have a specific assignment with the CDEA?

A: I head up the meth task force for the southern part of the state.

Q: How long have you had that assignment?

A: Five years.

. . .

Q: Did you have occasion to search the home of Mr. Rodney Mack?

A: Yes. I and other law enforcement officers went to Rodney Mack's residence in Kellogg, Columbia, to execute a search warrant.

1   **Q:** Did you find anything?

2   **A:** Yes. We found one-quarter pound of methamphetamine inside a vehicle and seized

3   methamphetamine, marijuana, drug records, cash, and drug paraphernalia from the

4   house.

5   **Q:** Did you have occasion to search the home of Mr. Tom Cord?

6   **A:** Law enforcement officers executed a search warrant at Cord's residence in Newton,

7   Columbia.

8   **Q:** Was anything seized?

9   **A:** Officers seized one-quarter pound of methamphetamine from the residence.

10 **Q:** Did you ask Mr. Cord about this?

11 **A:** Yes. He said he paid defendant $4,200 for the one-quarter pound of

12 methamphetamine.

13 **Q:** Did you find anything else?

14 **A:** We found a piece of paper with the name "Dolly" and defendant's phone number on

15 it. Cord said he had received the paper from Rodney Mack. Mack gave Cord

16 defendant's phone number so that Cord would always have a way to get in touch with

17 Dolan.

18 **Q:** Did you have occasion to search the defendant's home?

19 **A:** Yes. A few days later law enforcement officers executed a search warrant at

20 defendant's residence.

21 **Q:** What did you find?

22 **A:** Twelve firearms — four handguns and eight long guns — were seized from

23 defendant's residence. All twelve firearms were manufactured outside of Columbia.

24 Subsequent investigation showed that the Remington 12-gauge shotgun seized at one

25 time belonged to Rodney Mack.

26 **Q:** Was anything else seized?

27 **A:** Yes. Officers also seized 40 grams of methamphetamine from defendant's property.

28 **Q:** Where did you find this meth?

29 **A:** The methamphetamine was wrapped up and lying beside an ammunition can outside

30 on defendant's property alongside a driveway or lane 150 yards from defendant's

31 house.

32

1   **Q:** Did you seize anything else?

2   **A:** Some of the meth was laid out in a line next to a snort tube and a baggie containing

3   meth residue with a rubber band around it.

4   **Q:** Anything else?

5   **A:** Officers also seized around 73 pounds of marijuana. The majority of the marijuana

6   was in six large black garbage bags inside a locked 55-gallon drum. The drum was

7   buried on defendant's property. Also in the drum was a PVC pipe containing finely

8   manicured or processed marijuana. The drum was locked with a padlock and the key to

9   it was seized from the kitchen area of defendant's residence.

10 **Q:** And tell me about the key.

11 **A:** The key was not in the lock. Obviously, we wouldn't have used bolt cutters if it had

12 been. The key was secured from inside Mr. Dolan's residence a little bit later.

13 . . .

14 **Q:** Showing you what is marked as State's Exhibit 1, do you recognize it?

15 **A:** Yes.

16 **Q:** How do you recognize it?

17 . . .

18 **Q:** Showing you what is marked as State's Exhibit 18, do you recognize it?

19 **A:** Yes.

20 **Q:** How do you recognize it?

21 . . .

22 **Q:** Your Honor, having laid the foundation with Officer Atwood, at this point the state

23 would like to introduce into evidence State's Exhibits 1 through 18, specifically Exhibits

24 1-12, weapons seized from defendant's residence; Exhibit 13, 40 grams of

25 methamphetamine seized from defendant's property; Exhibit 14, a snort tube and a

26 baggie containing meth residue; Exhibit 15, the rubber band with which the baggie was

27 covered; Exhibit 16, 73 pounds of marijuana seized from the defendant's property;

28 Exhibit 17, the PVC pipe containing processed marijuana seized from the defendant's

29 property; and Exhibit 18, the key to the marijuana drum that was seized from the kitchen

30 area of defendant's residence.

31 **BY THE COURT:** They are so admitted.

32 . . .

1 **BY MS. JORDAN:** Detective Atwood, referring to State's Exhibit 13, how is meth

2 usually sold on the street?

3 **A:** Methamphetamine is generally sold in rock or powder form.

4 **Q:** What would be a typical sale in terms of amount sold for personal use?

5 **A:** Usually it will be sold in quarter-gram units for $35.00 a unit.

6 **Q:** Would 40 grams be for personal use?

7 **A:** Absolutely not.

8 **Q:** Typically, what would be the quality of the meth sold on the street, what level of

9 purity?

10 **A:** It is usually in the range of 10 to 15% pure.

11 . . .

12 **Q:** Would 73 pounds of marijuana be for personal use?

13 **A:** Absolutely not. Personal use is three or four ounces.

14   CROSS-EXAMINATION BY MS. MAYER

15 **Q:** You interviewed Mr. Cord, correct?

16 **A:** Yes.

17 **Q:** You took a statement from him, didn't you?

18 **A:** Yes.

19 **Q:** In that statement Mr. Cord insisted he did not have any agreement with Mr. Dolan,

20 did he not?

21 **A:** That's correct.

22 . . .

23 **Q:** Isn't it true that the methamphetamine was approximately 150 yards from

24 defendant's house?

25 **A:** Yes.

26 . . .

27 **Q:** The marijuana that was seized was water damaged, correct?

28 **A:** Some of it.

29 **Q:** The water damage meant that that particular marijuana was not marketable, correct?

30 **A:** Yes.

31

32

REDIRECT EXAMINATION

2   **Q:** The meth that was found 150 yards from the defendant's house, where precisely

3   was it?

4   **A:** Alongside defendant's driveway or lane.

5   **Q:** What about the marijuana, where was it found?

6   **A:** The marijuana was found less than 100 yards from the residence.

7   **Q:** Where did you find the key?

8   **A:** The key to the marijuana was found in defendant's residence.

9   **Q:** How much of the marijuana was water damaged?

10   **A:** About 20 percent.

11   **Q:** Was the other 80 percent marketable?

12   **A:** Yes.

13   <u>EXAMINATION OF ANNETTE KAHLER</u>

14   Annette Kahler, a witness called by the state, first being duly sworn, testified as follows:

15   DIRECT EXAMINATION BY MS. JORDAN

16   **Q:** Would you tell us your name?

17   **A:** Annette Kahler.

18   **Q:** Where do you work?

19   **A:** I am a forensic chemist with the Columbia Drug Enforcement Administration.

20   **Q:** How long have you worked with CDEA?

21   **A:** Twenty years.

22   . . .

23   **Q:** Showing you what has been marked as State's Exhibit 13, do you recognize it?

24   **A:** Yes, it is the meth seized in this case that I tested.

25   **Q:** What results did your testing reveal?

26   **A:** I analyzed the substance and found it weighed slightly more than 40 grams and

27   contained 40% pure methamphetamine.

28   . . .

29   **BY MS. JORDAN:** The defense has no questions for Ms. Kahler.

30   **BY MS. MAYER:** The state rests its case-in-chief, Your Honor.

31

32

<u>EXAMINATION OF BRUCE DOLAN</u>

Bruce Dolan, a witness called by the Defendant, first being duly sworn, testified as follows:

DIRECT EXAMINATION BY MS. MAYER

Q: Would you tell us your name?

A: Bruce Dolan.

. . .

Q: Were you aware of the drugs that were found in this case?

A: I had no idea they were there.

Q: How is that possible?

A: Look, a bunch of that stuff was obviously hidden. This is a rural area. I can only imagine someone was using it as a hiding place. I'm out all day working, get home after dark. I guess someone just took advantage of my absence.

Q: What about the key?

A: You know, I have given that a lot of thought. I hate to say it, but it kind of makes me think it was Will Gardner and his sister that were hiding the stuff. They certainly kept coming out to the house and bugging me. I never locked the place up, so who knows, they probably decided to leave the key there just for convenience.

Q: Anything else lead you to that conclusion?

A: Well, from what I've heard here, Will and his sister were obviously dealing.

Q: How about all the guns?

A: I like to hunt. Like I said, it's rural.

. . .

CROSS-EXAMINATION BY MS. JORDAN

Q: Mr. Dolan, this isn't the first time you have been arrested, is it?

A: No.

Q: In fact, isn't it true that you were charged with selling marijuana to a minor?

BY MS. MAYER: Objection, Your Honor. Use of an arrest is improper impeachment. Likewise, the sale of marijuana charge led to a plea of guilty by Mr. Dolan to a misdemeanor of endangerment of a minor and hence, even the conviction is improper impeachment under Columbia Rule of Evidence 609.

1 **BY MS. JORDAN:** Your Honor, this is not going to impeachment. Rather it is relevant to

2 prove motive, opportunity, intent, plan, etc., under Columbia Rule of Evidence 404(b).

3 **BY THE COURT:** Objection overruled. Go ahead.

4 **BY MS. JORDAN:** Isn't it true that you were charged with selling marijuana to a minor?

5 **A:** Yes.

6 **Q:** You pleaded guilty to endangerment of a minor, correct?

7 **A:** Yes.

8 **Q:** An element of the crime you were charged with was intent to distribute?

9 **A:** Don't know about that.

10 **Q:** When you pleaded guilty to endangerment, you admitted you sold marijuana to a

11 minor, didn't you?

12 **A:** My lawyer just told me to plead guilty so I could go home.

13 **Q:** But the judge, before accepting your plea, asked you about the circumstances of the

14 crime, correct?

15 **BY MS. MAYER:** Objection, Your Honor. I renew my previous objection and now object

16 to the introduction of the conviction. This is improper impeachment under 609.

17 **BY MS. JORDAN:** Your Honor, this is not going to impeachment. The evidence is

18 relevant under 404(b).

19 **BY THE COURT:** I'll overrule the objection.

20 **BY MS. JORDAN:** Mr. Dolan, let me ask again, the judge, before accepting your plea,

21 asked you about the circumstances of the crime, correct?

22 **A:** I don't remember.

23 **Q:** But certainly after this incident, you knew marijuana was illegal, correct?

24 **A:** Of course.

25 **Q:** Just like I'm sure you know possession of meth was illegal, correct?

26 **A:** You'd have to be pretty stupid not to know that, right?

27 **Q:** You don't consider yourself stupid, I assume?

28 **A:** No, I don't.

29 . . .

30 **BY MS. MAYER:** Your Honor, the defense rests.

31 **BY MS. JORDAN:** The State has no other witnesses.

1 **BY THE COURT:** Thank you. Given the late hour, I think we will recess until tomorrow

2 at 9:30 a.m. At that point I will hear closing arguments. Good afternoon.

3

4

5

6

7

8

9

10

11

12

13

14

15

16

17

18

19

20

21

22

23

24

25

26

27

28

29

30

31

FEBRUARY 2012

California
Bar
Examination

Performance Test B
LIBRARY

STATE v. DOLAN

LIBRARY

Selected Provisions of the Columbia Penal Code

§ 200 General requirements of culpability

a. *Minimum requirements of culpability.* Except as provided in subsection c.(3) of this section, a person is not guilty of an offense unless he acted purposely, knowingly, recklessly or negligently, as the law may require, with respect to each material element of the offense.

b. *Kinds of culpability defined.*

(1) *Purposely.* A person acts purposely with respect to the nature of his conduct or a result thereof if it is his conscious object to engage in conduct of that nature or to cause such a result. A person acts purposely with respect to attendant circumstances if he is aware of the existence of such circumstances or he believes or hopes that they exist. "With purpose," "designed," "with design" or equivalent terms have the same meaning.

(2) *Knowingly.* A person acts knowingly with respect to the nature of his conduct or the attendant circumstances if he is aware that his conduct is of that nature, or that such circumstances exist, or he is aware of a high probability of their existence. A person acts knowingly with respect to a result of his conduct if he is aware that it is practically certain that his conduct will cause such a result. "Knowing," "with knowledge" or equivalent terms have the same meaning.

*   *   *   *   *

§ 840 Possession

Except as authorized by this subchapter, it shall be unlawful for any person knowingly to possess a controlled substance as defined in § 875.

§ 841(a) Possession with intent to distribute

Except as authorized by this subchapter, it shall be unlawful for any person knowingly — (1) to manufacture, distribute, dispense, or possess with intent to manufacture, distribute, or dispense, a controlled substance as defined in § 875.

….

*   *   *   *   *

§ 846 Attempt and conspiracy

Any person who attempts or conspires to commit any offense defined in this subchapter shall be subject to the same penalties as those prescribed for the offense, the commission of which was the object of the attempt or conspiracy.

*　*　*　*　*

§ 875 Controlled substances

Controlled substances include:

....

(13) Marijuana.

....

(38) Methamphetamine.

State v. Jones
Columbia Supreme Court (1995)

Mark Jones, Jimmy Don Winemiller, Jr., Keith Gunter, and Barbara Whitehead appeal their convictions for various drug-related offenses. Winemiller and Gunter also appeal their sentences. We affirm all convictions and sentences, except for Winemiller's conviction for possession with the intent to distribute methamphetamine in violation of Columbia Penal Code § 841(a)(1). As to that conviction, we reverse and remand for entry of judgment and resentencing for possession of methamphetamine in violation of Columbia Penal Code § 840.

To support a conspiracy conviction, the government must show that: a conspiracy existed for an illegal purpose; the defendant knew of the conspiracy; and the defendant knowingly joined in it. Whitehead, Jones, Gunter and Winemiller argue there was insufficient evidence supporting their conspiracy convictions; Whitehead also claims insufficient evidence in regard to her possession conviction. They assert that the basis for the jury verdicts was Jones' testimony and that his testimony was incredible because he was a paid informant, had been granted immunity, had trouble remembering some dates, and psychological testing indicated that he had a poor memory. The jury, however, was aware of these things, and it was for the jury, not this court, to weigh Jones' credibility. Moreover, as the court noted in denying the motions for judgments of acquittal, although Jones' testimony had some inconsistencies, his testimony was not so incredible when weighed with other corroborating evidence produced by the government.

We find merit, however, to Winemiller's challenge to the sufficiency of the evidence supporting his conviction for possession with the intent to distribute methamphetamine. Winemiller does not contest the fact that Drug Enforcement Administration Agent Bryant testified that a four-gram quantity of methamphetamine was a distributable amount, but argues that the government failed to present testimony that the methamphetamine weighed four grams or other evidence demonstrating his intent to distribute. At oral argument, the government noted that at sentencing Winemiller stipulated that the methamphetamine weighed 4.1 grams, but conceded that it "dropped the ball" because it failed to present testimony at trial concerning the weight of the methamphetamine. The government, however, argued there was sufficient evidence before the jury based on the testimony that the methamphetamine was 47% pure as compared to methamphetamine found on the street, which was generally in the range of 10-15% pure.

We disagree with the government. It is true that intent to distribute may be established by circumstantial evidence, including such things as quantity and purity and the presence of firearms, cash, packaging material, or other distribution paraphernalia. Moreover, we recognize that intent to distribute may be inferred solely from the possession of large quantities of narcotics. Proof, however, of possession of a small amount of a controlled substance, standing alone, is an insufficient basis from which an intent to distribute may be inferred.

Assuming, without deciding, that intent can also be inferred solely from the purity of a drug, we do not believe that 47% pure, standing alone, is sufficient to prove beyond a reasonable doubt that Winemiller intended to distribute the methamphetamine. Moreover, even if evidence of weight had been before the jury, the facts here do not bring into play the doctrine that possession of large quantities of drugs justifies the inference that the drugs are for distribution and not for personal use. Although Bryant testified that a four-gram quantity was not for personal use, he admitted that personal use varied among individuals and that his opinion was based on a comparison to a $25.00 quarter-gram unit, which was the starting dose for methamphetamine sold on the street. This case is unlike *People v. Ojeda,* in which this court held that an inference of intent to distribute could be drawn from possession of 7.1 kilograms of 88 to 91% pure methamphetamine.

Rather, this case is similar to *People v. White* and *People v. Franklin*. In *White,* this court found that 7.54 grams of cocaine, which would make 75 to 80 dosage units, was insufficient, standing alone, to support a conviction for possession with intent to distribute, even though as little as five grams has been held to be a distributable amount. In *Franklin*, this court found that 35 grams of 42% pure cocaine, standing alone, was insufficient evidence from which a jury could infer intent to distribute.

In both cases, because quantity or quantity and purity combined were insufficient to support a reasonable inference of intent to distribute, the courts looked to additional circumstances or evidence consistent with intent to distribute narcotics.

In *White*, this court found sufficient additional evidence because the cocaine was packaged in multiple packages and the defendant had wired a large amount of cash and had a revolver.

In contrast, in *Franklin* the court reversed convictions for possession with the intent to distribute because of the lack of additional evidence of intent. In *Franklin*, the cocaine was not packaged in a manner consistent with distribution and the government offered no evidence of distribution paraphernalia, amounts of cash, weapons, or other indicia of narcotics distribution.

In this case, we conclude that the government failed to produce sufficient additional evidence from which a jury could draw a reasonable inference that Winemiller intended to distribute the methamphetamine. As in *Franklin*, the drug was not packaged for resale, and the government did not introduce evidence of a large amount of unexplained cash or other distribution paraphernalia. We are aware that a rifle and a shotgun were found in the trunk of Winemiller's car. Further, because a firearm is generally considered a tool of the trade for drug dealers it is also evidence of intent to distribute. We do not believe, however, that a reasonable jury could infer that the unloaded rifle and shotgun found in the trunk of the car along with camping gear, which included duck calls and waders, were "tools" of the drug trade. Indeed, the searching officer testified that the rifle was sitting "on top of all kinds of camping gear as if [Winemiller] was out camping or hunting with the weapon."

Winemiller, however, does not go free. The common elements of all drug possession offenses are: (1) a specified controlled substance, in a sufficient quantity, and in a usable form; (2) possession, which may be physical or constructive, exclusive or joint; and (3) knowledge of the fact of possession and of the illegal character of the substance. Each of these elements may be established circumstantially. Because the jury found Winemiller guilty of possession with the intent to distribute, the jury necessarily found all the elements of simple possession in violation of Columbia Penal Code § 840. We thus reverse and remand for the entry of judgment accordingly and for resentencing on this lesser included offense, but otherwise affirm.

State v. Hach
Columbia Supreme Court (1998)

Francis "Butch" Hach ("Butch") was involved in cocaine use and dealing in Cooksville, Columbia, from the late 1980's until his arrest in 1997. He was indicted for conspiracy to distribute cocaine along with Anthony and Nicholas LaCorcia and his own son Carl Hach ("Carl").

Butch was tried and convicted by a jury in January 1998, and was sentenced to 240 months imprisonment. He raises a bevy of issues on appeal, asking that his conviction be reversed, or in the alternative, that his sentence be vacated or remanded. Carl pleaded guilty to the conspiracy and was sentenced to 188 months imprisonment.

The Haches lived in Cooksville, Columbia at the Cooksville Blacksmith Shop, which Butch owned. Beginning sometime in the late 1980's Butch and Carl began to purchase cocaine, first from Mark LaCorcia (now deceased), then from Nick LaCorcia, and after Nick was incarcerated, from the third LaCorcia brother, Tony. The LaCorcias also had a partner, Tom Sajenko, who frequently couriered drugs and money to and from the Haches.

The defendants received their cocaine at the Blacksmith Shop. The cocaine was weighed on Carl's scale, and delivered to the defendants in their respective bedrooms. The Haches sometimes resold the cocaine they obtained from the LaCorcias and Sajenko. Tony LaCorcia continued delivering cocaine to the Haches until May 1997, when law enforcement authorities executed a search warrant on the Blacksmith Shop. At that time, Carl agreed to cooperate with law enforcement. Due to Carl's cooperation, Tony LaCorcia was arrested by the authorities.

At the defendants' separate sentencing hearings, the trial court made factual findings concerning the amount of drugs attributable to the conspiracy and to Butch and Carl individually. The trial court attributed between 5.4 and 8.3 kilograms of cocaine to the conspiracy. It also held that based on the joint participation of the defendants, each was accountable for the entire amount.

Butch contends that the trial court erred in denying his motion for a judgment of acquittal. When a defendant avers a lack of sufficient evidence, the question both the trial court and this Court ask is whether evidence exists from which any rational trier of fact could have found the essential elements of the crime beyond a reasonable doubt.

To sustain a conspiracy conviction, the record must contain evidence showing that a conspiracy to distribute cocaine existed, and that Butch Hach knowingly participated in it. Butch maintains that while he bought, consumed and sold cocaine, he had no agreement with the LaCorcias and Sajenko to distribute what they sold him. If he is correct, his conviction must be reversed, because, as we have held, to demonstrate a conspiracy, the government must show proof of an agreement to commit a crime other than the crime that consists of the sale of cocaine itself. A simple agreement between a buyer and seller to exchange something of value for cocaine cannot alone constitute a conspiracy because such an agreement is itself the substantive crime.

Butch argues that his relationship with his suppliers — the LaCorcias and Tom Sajenko, and his son Carl — was just this type of arm's-length buyer-seller arrangement. Butch argues that his dealers never directed him to sell the cocaine they had sold him. He seeks to bolster his case by contending, for example, that Tom Sajenko never said to him "Butch, here's some cocaine. If you can't sell it, you don't have to pay for it." According to Butch, the absence of such facts indicates the absence of a conspiracy.

We may, however, look beyond the lack of explicit agreements and direct evidence to circumstantial evidence which tends to establish the conspiracy to distribute cocaine. In reviewing the record, we look for evidence of a prolonged and actively pursued course of sales coupled with the seller's actual knowledge and a shared stake in the buyer's illegal venture. We have identified four factors as particularly salient in determining whether a conspiracy existed, and whether a defendant knowingly participated in it: (1) the length of affiliation, (2) the established method of payment, (3) the extent to

75

which transactions were standardized, and (4) the demonstrated level of mutual trust. Although none of these factors is dispositive, if enough are present and point to a concrete, interlocking interest beyond individual buy-sell transactions, we will not disturb the fact-finder's inference that, at some point, the buyer-seller relationship developed into a cooperative venture.

The record shows that each of these factors existed in the relationship between Butch and his coconspirators, and that in the aggregate, the facts denote the concrete and interlocked interest. As to the length of affiliation, Butch bought cocaine from the LaCorcias and Tom Sajenko for seven years. In that time, the LaCorcias and Sajenko provided Butch with cocaine on a steady basis, sometimes providing amounts fit for more than personal consumption. When one of the sellers was incarcerated or indisposed, another in the group picked up the slack.

The transactions were also standardized; nearly every sale had certain hallmarks. Deliveries were made almost exclusively to the upstairs bedrooms at the Blacksmith Shop; they were routinely made on Wednesdays or Thursdays. Each time, the cocaine was measured out and weighed in Carl's bedroom on Carl's scale, whether he was present or not. The payments were sometimes made at the time of delivery, and sometimes made a few days later. Sajenko testified that on occasion, if Butch did not have enough cash, Sajenko would still give him the cocaine and would return for full remuneration later. Frequent and repeated transactions with an attendant established method of payment that includes a rudimentary form of credit can support a conspiracy conviction.

These routinized deliveries indicate the fourth factor, demonstrated level of mutual trust. Butch and Carl permitted Tom Sajenko free, unencumbered access into their living area at the Blacksmith Shop, where he was allowed to use Carl's scale to weigh the cocaine. After apportioning the drugs, Sajenko waited for Carl and Butch to join him so he could deliver them their drugs. The arrangement advanced all parties' interests — the sellers had a safe place to distribute their cocaine, and the buyers (Butch and Carl) literally had bedroom service. Immediately upon receiving the cocaine in the confines of their home, Butch and Carl either used it themselves, or cut it and repackaged it for sale.

The length of affiliation, established method of payment and routinized transactions present here also underscore this demonstrated level of mutual trust. When Nick LaCorcia was about to go to prison, he arranged for his brother Tony to continue an uninterrupted flow of cocaine to Butch. This saved Butch from having to find an alternative source and worry about problems attendant to creating a new buyer-supplier relationship. He maintained a continuous source of drugs for himself and his clients. Sajenko and the LaCorcias benefitted from having such reliable customers even in the face of the turnover in their operation.

Viewing the evidence in total, it is clear that the factors we have found salient for determining whether a conspiracy existed are present here. For the foregoing reasons, the judgment of the trial court is affirmed.

Closing Argument: State v. Dolan

Presented by Richard Parsons, State's Attorney

INTRODUCTION:

Good morning, Your Honor. The State has charged Mr. Dolan with three crimes. (1) The possession of methamphetamine and marijuana; (2) the possession with intent to distribute methamphetamine and marijuana; and (3) conspiracy to distribute methamphetamine and marijuana. The State must prove each element of these three charges beyond a reasonable doubt. After hearing the presentation of evidence and the examination of nine witnesses, including the Defendant Mr. Dolan, the State contends that it has met its burden of proof for each element of each of the three crimes. The State will address each charge in turn and reiterate the evidence that supports each element of each charge beyond a reasonable doubt.

Count 1: Possession of Methamphetamine and Marijuana

As to the possession of methamphetamine and marijuana, the state must show that the Defendant knowingly possessed a controlled substance. As the Court knows, marijuana and methamphetamine are classified as controlled substances under §875 of the Columbia Penal Code. "Knowingly" means that Mr. Dolan must have been aware that his conduct, the possession of methamphetamine and marijuana, or that he was aware of a high probability that he was in possession of controlled substances in the form of methamphetamine and marijuana.

The crime of possession can be broken down into two elements that Mr. Dolan must have knowingly satisfied. The first is being aware of the possession or being aware of the high risk of possession of the substances. The second is being aware of the high probability the substances are of a controlled nature.

I will address the second element first because it can be proven beyond a reasonable doubt from Mr. Dolan's own testimony that he knew marijuana and methamphetamines to be a controlled substance sic]. Mr. Dolan testified that after he was arrested for selling marijuana to a minor that he "of course" knew marijuana to be illegal. Similarly, when asked whether he knew that the possession of meth was illegal, Mr. Dolan answered, "You'd have to be pretty stupid not to know that, right?" and maintained that he did not consider himself stupid. Thus, Mr. Dolan has admitted knowledge that both marijuana and methamphetamine are illegal drugs, or controlled substances. His knowledge of the illegal nature of the drugs has been proven beyond a reasonable doubt.

The Columbia Supreme Court, in State v. Jones, has added the additional requirement to the knowledge that the substance is [sic] possessed is a controlled substance. That requirement is that the substance be in sufficient and usable form. Here, the quantity of marijuana and methamphetamine is beyond a reasonable doubt sufficient to constitute possession. 40 grams of methamphetamine and 73 pounds of marijuana were discovered. This is no trace amount and is sufficient quantity for the purposes of mere possession. Additionally, the usability of the controlled substance was testified to in the testimony of B.J. Atwood, a Detective with the Columbia Drug Enforcement Administration. Mr. Atwood conceded that while 20% of the marijuana found had sustained water damage and was therefore unmarketable and unusable; however, the remaining 80% of the marijuana, some 58.4 pounds of marijuana, remained marketable and therefore usable. The methamphetamine sustained no damage and was usable. The State has established beyond a reasonable doubt that the marijuana and methamphetamine discovered in this instance was of sufficient and usable quantity.

The first element of possession, that of being aware that one is in possession of the controlled substance or that one has a high probability of being in possession of the controlled substance has also been proven beyond a reasonable doubt. The Columbia Supreme Court in State v. Jones states that that possession may be constructive, exclusive or joint and that proof of such possession may be established circumstantially. The methamphetamine was discovered 150 yards from the Defendant's house and the marijuana was discovered less than 100 yards from the Defendant's residence according to the testimony of B.J. Atwood. The methamphetamine was found alongside a driveway on the defendant's property. The marijuana was discovered inside a drum on the defendant's property. That the drugs were found on the defendant's property goes to the defendant's constructive possession of the controlled substance.

Further bolstering the constructive possession of the marijuana is the fact that the marijuana was discovered buried in a locked drum, the key to which was inside the defendant's house. The marijuana found on the defendant's property is thus linked to the defendant's residence through the presence of the key in the defendant's home. Mr. Dolan maintains that the key must have been left there by Will Gardner and his sister, whom he also blames for the presence of the substantial quantity of marijuana found on his property. However, Mr. Dolan presents no convincing testimony as to why Will Gardner and his sister would choose to store marijuana on his property or leave the key to the vessel containing the marijuana in his residence other than he heard they were "obviously dealing." Mr. Dolan presents no evidence as to why the methamphetamine would be on his property, along is [sic] driveway, presumably in plain view. His testimony is unconvincing and uncorroborated. In fact, Mr. Dolan's testimony is directly contradicted by Lynette Rogers, Will Gardner's sister. Ms. Rogers testified that she and her brother frequently visited Mr. Dolan's residence to purchase drugs and Ms. Rogers' phone record shows that she made three calls to Mr. Dolan's home phone during a three-month period in late 2009. If Ms. Rogers and her brother were "obviously dealing," they were doing so with drugs obtained from Mr. Dolan on Mr. Dolan's property, a point that will be flushed out when we arrive at the count of conspiracy.

For now, the evidence has born[e] out that Mr. Dolan knew beyond a reasonable doubt that methamphetamine and marijuana were controlled substances and that Mr. Dolan had methamphetamine of sufficient quantity and usability to satisfy a charge of possession. Additionally, knowing possession has been establismed through Mr. Dolan's constructive possession of the marijuana and methamphetamine on his property, both in plain view in the case of the methamphetamine and in a locked container to which Mr. Dolan kept the key in his home in the case of the marijuana.

Count 2: Possession with intent to distribute methamphetamine and marijuana

The Columbia Supreme Court has stated in State v. Jones that intent to distribute may be established by circumstantial evidence, including such things as quantity and purity and the presence of firearms, cash, packaging material, or other distribution paraphernalia. The State has shown beyond a reasonable doubt that circumstantial evidence supporting a finding of intent to distribute is present in this case, including a PVC pipe containing finely manicured or processed marijuana, a snort tube and baggie containing meth residue, a rubber band with which that baggie was covered, and twelve firearms including four handguns and eight long guns, all produced outside the state of Columbia and one of which at one time belonged to Rodney Mack, a man who you heard testify to reselling the drugs Mr. Dolan sold to him.

The Columbia Supreme Court stated in Jones that intent to distribute can be inferred solely from the possession of large quantities of narcotics. Here, 40 grams of methamphetamine were seized on Mr. Dolan's property and 73 pounds of marijuana were seized on Mr. Dolan's property. The Columbia Supreme Court held in Jones that 4.1 grams of methamphetamine, standing alone, was insufficient to infer an intent to distribute. In People v. White, the Columbia Supreme Court found that 7.54 grams of cocaine, standing alone, was insufficient to infer an intent to distribute, and in People v. Franklin the court found that 35 grams of cocaine, standing alone, did not support an intent to distribute.

While cocaine is a drug separate and apart from methamphetamine and marijuana, the quantities deemed sufficient to infer an intent to distribute cocaine is informative to infer such an intent in this case. The 73 pounds of marijuana far exceeds any of the quantities deemed insufficient in Jones, White, or Franklin and is beyond a reasonable doubt a large enough quantity of marijuana to infer that Mr. Dolan was not keeping the marijuana on his property for personal use. Jones, White, and Franklin also permit evidence other than quantity to be considered when finding an intent to distribute. With regard to the marijuana, beyond the large quantity discovered, the court should also consider the PVC pipe that contained processed marijuana. That the defendant was

81

processing marijuana from bulk quantities indicates an intent to distribute. Moreover, the fact that the marijuana was kept in bulk, in 6 large garbage bags, buried under Mr. Dolan's property, also indicates that the marijuana was not on hand merely for personal use. It was being kept in the ground to await processing by Mr. Dolan for distribution. The quantity and supplemental evidence are enough to show beyond a reasonable doubt that the marijuana possessed by Mr. Dolan was intended for distribution.

As to the methamphetamine, the 40 grams of methamphetamine far exceeds the 4.1 grams and 7.54 grams of cocaine deemed insufficient in Jones and White. However, given the finding in Franklin that 35 grams was insufficient, standing alone, to find an intent to distribute, this court must look to other evidence outside of quantity to determine that Defendant had an intent to distribute methamphetamine. The court may look to the purity of the controlled substance. The methamphetamine discovered on Mr. Dolan's property was 40%, as testified to by Annette Kahler of the Columbia Drug Enforcement Administration. Mr. Atwood testified that methamphetamine for distribution was around 10 to 15% pure, indicating that the methamphetamine possessed by Defendant was intended to be processed and broken down, not intended for personal use but rather for distribution. However, the Court in Franklin found that 42% purity in cocaine found in a 35 gram quantity was insufficient to show an intent to distribute.

The court then must look to other evidence to supplement the large quantity and high purity of the methamphetamine found on Mr. Dolan's property in order to make a finding of intent to distribute beyond a reasonable doubt. Mr. Dolan had in his possession a snort tube and baggie containing meth residue covered in a rubber band as well as 12 firearms. The snort tube and baggie may be evidence of Mr. Dolan's personal usage, but they are also evidence that Mr. Dolan had methamphetamine at one time that was of a usable purity, indicating that Mr. Dolan had in fact broken down the high purity methamphetamine he possessed so much of for personal usage. In addition, the baggie and rubber band indicate that Mr. Dolan was packaging the usable methamphetamine, and packaging, as the court in White held, is indicative of distribution.

Perhaps most damning is the presence of the 12 firearms. The Court in State v. Jones found that an unloaded rifle and shotgun found in the trunk of a car alongside camping gear and hunting paraphernalia could not be classified as "tools" of the drug trade. Mr. Dolan contends that his firearms were also used for hunting and pointed to his rural residence as evidence of his hunting hobby. However, beyond being located in a rural area, Mr. Dolan presents no evidence that he engages in recreational hunting. Unlike in Jones, Mr. Dolan's firearms were not found among duck callers and camping gear. Additionally, Mr. Dolan possessed four handguns, which are not used in recreational hunting. The sheer quantity of the firearms Mr. Dolan possessed, when found alongside such large quantities of drugs, support the inference that Mr. Dolan possessed his firearms as "tools of the drug trade." To further prove this point, none of the firearms were manufactured inside the state of Columbia. Why would Mr. Dolan be in possession of so many out-of-state firearms, including handguns, and have such large quantities of controlled substances if he were not involved in the business of distributing drugs?

The large quantity, high purity, unprocessed nature of the drugs found on Mr. Dolan's property, along with the firearms, packaging materials, and drug paraphernalia support a finding beyond a reasonable doubt that Mr. Dolan was involved in the trade of drugs and the finding that Mr. Dolan possessed methamphetamine and marijuana with an intent to distribute.

Count 3: Conspiracy to distribute methamphetamine and marijuana

As to the count of conspiracy to distribute methamphetamine and marijuana, the State must prove beyond a reasonable doubt the elements of conspiracy laid out in the Columbia Supreme Court case State v. Jones. The State contends that it has proven the foregoing elements from State v. Jones beyond a reasonable doubt. (1) A conspiracy existed for an illegal purpose; (2) the Defendant, Mr. Dolan, knew of the conspiracy; and (3) the Defendant, Mr. Jones, knowingly joined in it.

To prove each of these elements, the State must first show beyond a reasonable doubt that a conspiracy in fact existed.

While the Columbia Supreme Court stated in State v. Hach that "a simple agreement between buyer and seller to exchange something of value for cocaine cannot alone constitute a conspiracy," the State has shown beyond a reasonable doubt that Mr. Dolan's drug transactions were more expansive than individual agreements and were in fact a conspiracy.

As the Court stated in State v. Hach, a conspiracy agreement can be shown by circumstantial evidence, including evidence of a prolonged and actively pursued course of sales coupled with the seller's actual knowledge and a shared stake in the buyer's illegal venture. The four factors the Court establishes in Hach to prove the existence of a conspiracy are: (1) the length of the affiliation; (2) the established method of payment; (3) the extent to which transactions were standardized; and (4) the demonstrated level of mutual trust. Evidence presented at trial has proven each of these conspiracy elements beyond a reasonable doubt.

With regard to the length of the affiliation, Rodney Mack testified that he bought drugs from Mr. Dolan for over two years between the period of June 2008 and October 2010 and has known Mr. Dolan since high school. In fact, Mr. Dolan and Mr. Mack were close friends in high school, hanging out together, drinking together, even being arrested together. Mr. Crutchfield testified that he has known Mr. Dolan for 10 years. Mr. Cord has known Mr. Dolan for 10 years, also from high school, and contends that he bought drugs from Mr. Dolan for resale for over a year, between June 2009 and December 2010. The affiliation between the Defendant and these men has existed since for ten plus years, as far back as high school, and the period of drug sale for resale between Mr. Dolan and these men was between one and two years. Without a doubt, there is a close affiliation between these three men that has continued for a lengthy period of time.

As to the established method of payment, you hear Mr. Mack testify that Mr. Dolan was "very rigid" in his payment methods: "cash only, nothing larger than $20 bills. No negotiation on price. Strictly take it or leave it." Mr. Cord echoed this payment method to a T, testifying that the method was "Cash only, nothing larger than $20 bills. He would get really angry is [sic] you tried to negotiate the price. He always said, "Take it or leave it." Ms. Rogers also testified to this transaction method, stating "He would only accept $20 bills," and he was "very clear" he would not negotiate on price. This corroborating testimony from three separate witnesses establishes beyond a reasonable doubt that Mr. Dolan had an established method of payment.

As to the standardization of the transactions, evidence has been presented that demonstrates that these transactions were extremely standardized. Mr. Mack testified that Mr. Dolan "had really strict rules" about the transactions and would only sell at his house or in the Tama casino. Mr. Crutchfield testified that he accompanied Mr. Mack to the Tama casino to pick up methamphetamines, corroborating Mr. Mack's testimony. Mr. Cord testified that he would purchase from Mr. Dolan at his house or at the Tama casino. Ms. Rogers testified to buying from Mr. Dolan at his residence or the Tama casino and Ms. Black testified that she accompanied Mr. Cord to Mr. Mack's house to buy drugs, corroborating Mr. Cord's testimony. Every witness called against Mr. Dolan who was involved in a drug transaction having to do with Mr. Dolan testifies to this transaction. It is beyond a reasonable doubt an extremely standardized transaction method.

Finally, the State must show that there was mutual trust between the parties to establish the presence of a conspiracy. Beyond the mere fact that each individual involved in these transactions knew of Mr. Dolan's link to the sale of drugs and each affectionately knew of Mr. Dolan's nickname, Dolly, other evidence exists to show that mutual trust between the parties existed beyond a reasonable doubt. Mr. Dolan primarily sold Mr. Mack and Mr. Cord drugs for them to resell, per their testimony, for a two year and a one year period respectively, a steady basis that State. v. Hach classifies as an indication of a conspiracy. These parties testified to knowing Mr. Dolan since high school, with Mr. Mack being particularly close friends with Mr. Dolan and Mr. Cord, continuing to be close friends with Mr. Mack. There exists a mutuality of trust between these friends. Mr. Dolan was even found to be in possession of one of Mr. Mack's old guns, another demonstration of the trust between these two men. Although Mr. Cord told Detective Atwood that he had no agreement with Mr. Dolan for the resale of drugs, the two continued their relationship, per Mr. Cord's testimony, under the understanding that Mr. Dolan "used his friends to actually distribute drugs." Mr. Crutchfield even testified that when either Mr. Cord or Mr. Mack was not available to sell drugs, he would just purchase drugs from the other. This "picking up the slack" between parties to drug transactions is cited by State v. Hach as evidence of a conspiracy.

Mr. Dolan also sold drugs to Mr. Gardner for redistribution according to the testimony of Ms. Rogers, Mr. Gardner's sister. Mr. Dolan himself corroborates that Mr. Gardner and his sister were in the business of selling drugs, noting that Will and his sister were "obviously drug dealing." Mr. Dolan himself indicates the level of trust he had with Mr. Gardner and his sister, noting that the pair would keep "coming out to the house and bugging me," and that he "never locked the place up." In State v. Hach, the court found that "free, unencumbered access to living areas" was evidence of mutual trust. That Mr. Dolan would invite drug buyers to his house which he admits he never locks up is a testament to his trust for the individuals to whom he sold.

The above demonstrations standardized payment, standardized transactions, longevity, and mutual trust between a group of people that Mr. Mack testified to being "a close-knit group of friends and neighbors," all "related in one way or another," is evidence beyond a reasonable doubt under the elements set forth in State v. Hach that a conspiracy existed beyond a reasonable doubt.

Mr. Dolan voluntarily engaged in the sale of drugs to this network of individuals, and as the above evidence has established that this network of transactions constitutes a conspiracy, Mr. Dolan was beyond a reasonable doubt voluntarily involved and in agreement with that conspiracy.

CONCLUSION:

The State has shown beyond a reasonable doubt that Mr. Dolan knowingly possessed controlled substances in satisfaction of the possession charge. The State has also shown beyond a reasonable doubt by use of circumstantial evidence that Mr. Dolan intended to distribute these controlled substances. He had large, unprocessed quantities of the substances as well as drug and packaging paraphernalia and 12 firearms consistent with "tools of the drug trade." Finally, the State has established the existence of a conspiracy by proving beyond a reasonable doubt that such a conspiracy existed given the longevity of the relationships between those involved, the established method of payment, the standardization of the transaction, and the demonstrated level of mutual trust between the participants.

The defense will offer no evidence to shed any doubt on the above proofs. In fact, all the defense can maintain is that the witnesses testifying against Mr. Dolan are biased. Biased because they have cut deals with the prosecutor to reduce their sentence for their own party in Mr. Dolan's drug conspiracy or biased because a close relative has died as a result of drug use. However, taken in their totality, the testimonies of these witnesses are corroborative and persuasive. Each echoes the story of the other to such an extent that any bias that may exist may be ignored. Bias does not cause witnesses to echo one another's stories so precisely. Bias does not alter the length and quality of the relationships between those testifying and Mr. Dolan.

Possession has been established. Intent to distribute has been established. Conspiracy has been established. All three charges and each of their individual elements have been established beyond a reasonable doubt. The State has met its burden of proof and Mr. Dolan should be convicted of possession, intent to distribute, and conspiracy.

Thank you.

Draft of Closing Argument - State v. Dolan

Your Honor, based on the evidence presented in this trial, the State has proven beyond a reasonable doubt that the Defendant, Bruce Dolan, should be convicted of: (1) possession of methamphetamine and marijuana under Section 840 of the Columbia Penal Code; (2) possession with intent to distribute methamphetamine and marijuana under Section 841(a) of the Columbia Penal Code; and (3) conspiracy to distribute methamphetamine and marijuana under Section 846 of the Columbia Penal Code. The overwhelming evidence against Mr. Dolan that has been presented -- including, without limitation, the uncovering of 40 grams of 40% pure methamphetamine and 73 pounds of marijuana on defendant's property and the testimony of multiple witnesses that Mr. Dolan has distributed methamphetamine and marijuana over a period of years -- establishes each element of the above charges beyond a reasonable doubt.

First, the State has proven that Mr. Dolan should be convicted of possession of methamphetamine and marijuana.

In order for Mr. Dolan to be convicted of possession of methamphetamine and marijuana under Section 840 of the Columbia Penal Code, it must be shown that Mr. Dolan knowingly possessed a controlled substance as defined in Section 875 of the Columbia Penal Code. The Columbia Supreme Court in State v. Jones has expanded upon these elements, such that the following showing is required: (1) a specified controlled substance, in a sufficient quantity, and in a useable form; (2) possession, which may be physical or constructive, exclusive or joint; and (3) knowledge of the possession and of the illegal character of the substance. Per the Jones decision, each of these elements may be established circumstantially. Under the Columbia Penal Code, a person acts knowingly with respect to the nature of his conduct or the attendant circumstances if he is aware that his conduct is of that nature, or if such circumstances exist, or he is aware of a high probability of their existence.

88

First, this case involves the possession of controlled substances, as per statute, Section 875 of the Columbia Penal Code provides that both marijuana and methamphetamine are controlled substances. This is confirmed by the testimony of Annette Kahler, a forensic chemist with the Columbia Drug Enforcement Administration, who testified that the substances found on Defendant's property comprised 40 grams of methamphetamine. Further, Detective Atwood testified that 73 pounds of marijuana was contained in a drum that was buried on Defendant's property. These are both in a sufficient quantity, as the statute does not provide any specific quantity is required -- thus, the mere possession of any amount of the controlled substances suffices. Further, both the methamphetamine and marijuana was [sic] in a useable form. Defendant's counsel may make the argument that part of the marijuana was water damaged; however, the majority of the marijuana, 80%, was marketable according to the testimony of Detective Atwood. Thus, the first element of possession is clearly established with respect to both methamphetamine and marijuana.

Second, it is clear that Defendant possessed the methamphetamine and marijuana. According to the Jones decision, possession may be physical or constructive, exclusive or joint. This element is satisfied to the extent that both methamphetamine and marijuana were stored and contained on Defendant's property. The methamphetamine was found wrapped up on Defendant's property approximately 150 yards from Defendant's house. The marijuana was located in a buried drum on Defendant's property, which was locked with a padlock with the key to the padlock located in the kitchen of Defendant's residence.

Third, it is clear that the Defendant has knowledge of the possession and illegal character of the methamphetamine and marijuana. It is no surprise that these drugs were located at Defendant's premises, as multiple witnesses testified that they purchased drugs at Defendant's house. Rodney Mack testified that he purchased methamphetamine at Defendant's house for over a two-year period from June 2008 through September or October 2010. Tom Cord also testified that he purchased drugs from the Defendant at Defendant's residence. Tom Cord's testimony was confirmed by Stacey Black's testimony, as she testified that Tom purchased drugs at Defendant's house on two occasions, and witnessed the drugs first-hand. Further, Lynette Rogers testified that methamphetamine was purchased at the Defendant's house. Thus, while Defendant has purported that Will Gardner and his sister, Lynette Rogers, were hiding the drugs at his residence, there is no evidence whatsoever to back up his position. In addition, Defendant may wish to assert that a conviction may not be sustained on the basis of testimony of being granted that Rodney Mack and Tom Cord stand to receive reduced sentences in connection with their testimony in the present case. However, we note that other witnesses who are not receiving a similar incentive are testifying to the same fact that drugs have been purchased in the past at Defendant's house. Moreover, Jones stands for the proposition that it is the role of the fact-finder to weigh credibility, and based on the other corroborating evidence and witness testimony, the overwhelming evidence shows that Defendant knew that methamphetamine and marijuana was [sic] located on his premises.

Finally, it is clear that Defendant knew that methamphetamine and marijuana were illegal substances, as he admitted such during cross-examination.

Thus, the elements of possession have been satisfied, and Mr. Dolan should clearly be convicted of possession of methamphetamine and marijuana.

Next, Mr. Dolan should also be convicted of possession with intent to distribute methamphetamine and marijuana.

A conviction for possession for intent to distribute methamphetamine and marijuana must meet the elements of Section 841(a) of the Columbia Penal Code, such that it shall be unlawful for any person knowingly to manufacture, distribute, dispense, or possess with intent to manufacture, distribute, or dispense, a controlled substance as defined in Section 875 of the Columbia Penal Code. Note that simple possession is required for conviction of an intent to distribute, which was previously discussed. In Jones, the Columbia Supreme Court held that the intent to distribute may be established by circumstantial evidence, including such things as quantity and purity of the controlled substance, the presence of firearms, cash, packaging material, or other

90

distribution paraphernalia. In addition, the Jones court held that intent to distribute may be inferred solely from the possession of large quantities of narcotics.

First, it is clear in this case that the storing of 73 pounds of marijuana satisfies the requirement that intent to distribute may be inferred solely from the large amount that Defendant was storing. Further to the testimony of Detective Atwood, personal use of marijuana is typically three to four ounces. Intent to distribute is also supported by the PVC pipe containing processed marijuana, evincing an intent to distribute rather than for personal use. Finally, Defendant was charged in the past with selling marijuana to a minor, and Defendant pleaded guilty to a lesser charge of endangerment of a minor where Defendant likely admitted selling marijuana to a minor. Thus, the mere quantity of marijuana alone is sufficient to support a reasonable inference of intent to distribute.

With respect to the methamphetamine, a number of factors support the position that Defendant had the intent to distribute the methamphetamine. First, we note that the holding in Jones provides that 4.1 grams of 47% pure methamphetamine, standing alone, is insufficient to prove intent to distribute methamphetamine. However, this case is distinguishable, to the extent that approximately 10 times the amount of methamphetamine is present in this case -- over 40 grams -- at a similar level of purity (40%). Thus, this case is more analogous to People v. Ojeda, in which the Columbia Supreme Court held that an inference of intent to distribute could be drawn from a possession of 7.1 kilograms of 88 to 91% pure methamphetamine. However, even if the court does not agree that such an inference should be drawn, the Jones court stated that, where the amount and purity of the drug were insufficient to support intent to distribute, the courts look to additional factors or circumstances consistent to intent to distribute. There are multiple factors here to support intent to distribute methamphetamine. First, there is a large amount of methamphetamine at a purity level approximately three to four times greater than what is sold on the street. Second, there is a common scheme and method of operation of past instances where the Defendant distributed methamphetamine in the past, both at his house and at the casino in Tama. Thus, it is reasonable to assume that Defendant would also distribute this methamphetamine. Third, there is a huge volume of marijuana, suggesting a common plan to distribute both drugs. Finally, there is the presence of 12 firearms seized from the Defendant's residence, which are tools of the drug trade. Defendant may purport that he uses these weapons for hunting; however, there is no evidence that Defendant presented demonstrating other hunting gear to support this fanciful position, and the fact that there were 4 handguns in addition to 8 long guns makes it implausible that the guns were all being used for hunting purposes, but rather as protection for his drug venture.

Thus, based on the overwhelming evidence, the State has proven beyond a reasonable doubt that Mr. Dolan should be convicted of possession with intent to distribute methamphetamine and marijuana.

Finally, Mr. Dolan should be convicted of conspiracy to distribute methamphetamine and marijuana.

Pursuant to the Columbia Supreme Court's decision in Jones, a conviction for conspiracy requires the government to show that: (1) a conspiracy existed for an illegal purpose; (2) the defendant knew of the conspiracy; and (3) the defendant knowingly joined in it. In turn, in a later Columbia Supreme Court decision, State v. Hach, the Columbia Supreme Court stated that a conspiracy conviction shall be sustained where the record contains evidence showing that a conspiracy existed, and that the defendant knowingly participated in it. Further, the Hach court stated that the government must show proof of an agreement to commit a crime other than the crime that consists of the sale of a controlled substance itself; however, an explicit agreement or direct evidence is not required to show that a conspiracy existed, and circumstantial information may be used, such as a prolonged and actively pursued course of sales, along with the seller's actual knowledge and a shared stake in the illegal venture. Four factors are used to determine whether there is a conspiracy: (a) the length of affiliation between the parties involved; (b) whether there is an established method of payment; (c) the extent to which the transactions were standardized; and (d) the demonstrated level of mutual trust. In Hach, the court viewed all the evidence in total, and found that these factors supported a finding of a conspiracy.

Similar to Hach, we have analogous factors in our case to support a finding of a conspiracy to distribute methamphetamine and marijuana. At the outset, per the testimony of Todd Bram, Mr. Bram stated that the Defendant knew that there was a plan to resell the drugs by Will Gardner, and that Defendant told Todd that "he did not do retail," and that he should buy the drugs from Will Gardner. This evidences directly that the Defendant knowingly joined in the conspiracy to have drugs resold on the retail market to his suppliers. This is further supported by the fact that Lynette Rogers got to know the Defendant through her boyfriend, Billy Purvis, who purchased methamphetamine from Rodney Mack, and knew that he acquired the methamphetamine from Defendant.

With respect to the Defendant's coconspirators, there was an established length of affiliation between the parties. In the case of Rodney Mack, there were sales for over two years, from June 2008 through September or October 2010. In the case of Tom Cord, he purchased drugs from the Defendant over a one-and-a-half year period from June 2009 through December 2010. Lynette Rogers also testified to a similar scheme where drugs were purchased at multiple times, supported by cell phone records showing calls to the Defendant's residence to support this position.

Next, there was also an established method of payment between the Defendant and his purchasers. Multiple witnesses testified that the Defendant accepted cash only, in bill amounts no greater than $20, and that the price was non-negotiable, and that Defendant made clear that these were strict rules that his purchasers needed to follow.

Third, there were standardized transactions. All of the transactions were made at Defendant's home or at the Tama casino. Defendant's knowledge and acceptance of the conspiracy is further supported by the testimony of Richard Crutchfield, who stated that he purchased methamphetamine from Tom Cord and Rodney Mack at the Tama casino, and Mr. Mack would leave the casino to pick up the methamphetamine, which Mr. Mack testified came from the Defendant.

Finally, there was a demonstrated level of mutual trust between Defendant and his purchasers who resold the drugs. All of these people had long-standing relationships with Defendant, and referred to him by a nickname, "Dolly," the name he was known by his friends. Per the testimony of Mr. Mack, Defendant only sold to a close-knit group of friends and neighbors, which primarily consisted of persons with whom Defendant went to high school. In sum, the arrangement advanced all the participants' interests -- Defendant could keep a role as a wholesaler of the drugs, while his close friends would resell the drugs on the open market.

Thus, in light of the Hach decision and the above factors, Mr. Dolan should be convicted of conspiracy.

Based on the foregoing, Your Honor, the State respectfully requests that you find the Defendant, Bruce Dolan, guilty of possession, intent to distribute, and conspiracy to distribute methamphetamine and marijuana.